Berwick-upon-Tweed

Three places, two nations, one town

Berwick-upon-Tweed

Three places, two nations, one town

Adam Menuge with Catherine Dewar

Published by English Heritage, Kemble Drive, Swindon SN2 2GZ
www.english-heritage.org.uk
English Heritage is the Government's statutory adviser on all aspects of the historic environment.

First published 2009
Reprinted 2011

ISBN 978 1 84802 029 0
Product code 51471

British Library Cataloguing in Publication Data
A CIP catalogue record for this book is available from the British Library.

The National Monuments Record is the public archive of English Heritage. For more information, contact NMR
Enquiry and Research Services, National Monuments Record Centre, Kemble Drive, Swindon SN2 2GZ;
telephone (01793) 414600.

Typeset in ITC Charter 9.25 on 13pt

Photographs by Bob Skingle and Adam Menuge
Aerial photographs by David MacLeod
Graphics by Allan T Adams and Philip Sinton
Brought to publication by Rachel Howard, Publishing, English Heritage
Edited by René Rodgers, Publishing, English Heritage
Page layout by George Hammond
Printed in Belgium by DeckersSnoeck

Northumberland County Council has made a financial contribution to the publication of this book.

Front cover
Berwick Bridge, built 1611–34,
entered what was then still a heavily
fortified town from the south; the
18th- and 19th-century granaries
and houses rising above the Quay
Walls reflect the town's important
seaborne trade and the prosperity
that it brought.
[DP071102]

Frontispiece
The defence of the town and the
prosperity of its trade were objectives
often at odds with one another.
Between Bridge Street, where many of
Berwick's merchants had their
businesses, and the Quay, on which
they relied for the movement of goods,
a series of lanes and tunnels were
created through the ramparts, which
would otherwise have strangled the
commercial life of the town.
[DP065192]

Contents

Acknowledgements

This book forms part of English Heritage's contribution to a wider collaboration with partners seeking to reconcile Berwick's need to develop a vibrant, modern economy with the obligation to respect its unique heritage. We are grateful to our partners on the Berwick's Future initiative – Berwick-upon-Tweed Borough Council, especially Shona Alexander, Director of Regeneration & Development; Berwick-upon-Tweed Town Council; Berwick Community Trust; Government Office for the North East; Northumberland County Council; Northumberland Strategic Partnership; One NorthEast; and the Local Strategic Partnership – for their continued support.

The photographs in this book have been specially taken by Bob Skingle with the exception of the image on p vii, Figs 3, 7, 23, 58, 59, 84a, 91, 102, 106 and 107 which were taken by Adam Menuge and Fig 112 which was taken by Catherine Dewar. The aerial photographs are by David MacLeod except Figs 18, 36, 62, 71, 78 and 98. The drawn figures are the work of Allan T Adams (Figs 17, 52, 63a and 85) and Philip Sinton (inside front cover, p 114 and inside back cover). Figs 15, 81, 87 and 89 are reproduced by permission of Berwick-upon-Tweed Record Office where we extend particular thanks to Linda Bankier and Carole Pringle for knowledgeable advice and generous assistance. Figs 27, 51 and 95 are included by permission of Berwick-upon-Tweed Museum & Art Gallery, where Chris Green and Jim Herbert gave similar support. For permission to photograph the Town Hall and its museum (Figs 43, 44, 45, 46, 50, 54 and 94), and for advice on its contents, we are indebted to Liam Henry (Clerk to the Berwick-upon-Tweed Corporation (Freemen) Trustees) and Michael Herriott (Curator and Guide). Robin Harcourt Williams (Librarian and Archivist) and Vicki Perry (Assistant Archivist) at Hatfield House made available Fig 24, which appears by kind permission of the Marquess of Salisbury. Other illustrations appear with the permission of the Bodleian Library (Fig 4), Bridgeman Art Library (Fig 35a), British Library (Figs 14, 28, 49 and 75) and The National Archives (Figs 13 and 103).

For further invaluable assistance, advice and expertise relating to aspects of Berwick's architecture and history we are especially grateful to Francis Cowe (Berwick resident and historian) who, together with Linda Bankier, commented helpfully on the text; Andrea Kirkham (independent wallpainting specialist); Margaret Richardson (Lutyens Trust); Canon Alan Hughes (Vicar of Holy Trinity Church) who kindly allowed us to photograph his 1761 *Book of Common Prayer* (Fig 6); Annette Reeves and Peter Rutherford (Berwick-upon-Tweed Borough Council); John Smithson (Berwick Preservation Trust); Harry Beamish (The National Trust); Wendy Lynch (King's Arms Hotel); and Gavin Cairns (Freeman) for making a copy of James Good's rare *Directory* available on the web.

Residents of Berwick, Tweedmouth and Spittal – many of them members of Berwick Civic Society and Berwick Historical Society, and of the Berwick Building Recording Group, newly formed in pursuit of the town's architectural research potential – have given invaluable support. Special thanks are offered to Alison, John and William Cowe, Lady Zoreen Hill, Ian Kille, David Mayers, Philip Miller, Judy Nicholson, Christopher and Do Shaw, Peter and Margaret Thomas, Jim Walker and to Councillors Hazel Bettison (last Mayor of Berwick Borough) and Peter Watts (Berwick-upon-Tweed Borough Council's Heritage Champion).

Numerous debts within English Heritage must also be acknowledged. The early part of the project was undertaken in conjunction with Matthew Withey, while Allison Borden, Garry Corbett and Lucy Jessop assisted with later fieldwork. Lucy Jessop also undertook valuable work securing illustrative material. Clare Broomfield and Emma Whinton-Brown in the NMR, together with Katy Whitaker and Angharad Wicks (Aerofilms Collection, NMR), helped in the provision of archive images. For other collaboration and encouragement thanks are offered to Kate Bould, Nick Bridgland, John Cattell, Rachel Cross, Colum Giles, Bob Hawkins, Rachel Howard, Matthew Oakey, Paul Pattison, Carol Pyrah, Sally Radford, Martin Roberts, René Rodgers, Malcolm Sutcliffe, Myra Tolan-Smith and Humphrey Welfare.

Places are composed of innumerable buildings and other features, but they are also bound together by ties, some tangible like the two road bridges linking Berwick and Tweedmouth, some intangible like the bonds formed by common building materials or patterns of trade and ownership. [NMR 20688/11]

Foreword

Towns are among the most impressive, intricate and enduring human achievements. They are artefacts on a grand scale – the outcome in most cases of centuries of effort, both collaborative and competitive – and like other artefacts they can be damaged by careless handling. Yet towns must continue to change if they are to meet the needs of future generations, and for this reason they will remain a focus for debate and sometimes contention. Meeting present needs and planning for the future, while respecting the character and significance of what the past has left behind, is a considerable challenge and a characteristically modern dilemma.

Nikolaus Pevsner described Berwick-upon-Tweed as 'one of the most exciting towns in England'[1] – a place where an absorbing historical tale can still be read in the dense fabric of its streets and buildings. It attracts not only holidaymakers but also new residents who have learnt to appreciate its special atmosphere. But outsiders all too easily confine their attention to the space within the impressive Elizabethan ramparts, while local people are sometimes unaware or dismissive of the wider significance of the very things that they know so intimately.

Berwick deserves to be known better and to be celebrated not just as a vivid reminder of what many other towns were once like, but more especially as something unique and distinctive, shaped by a peculiar combination of historical and geographical circumstances. This distinctiveness is acutely apparent as one passes between Berwick and the contrasting, but historically intertwined, settlements of Tweedmouth and Spittal.

Understanding Berwick's historic environment is all the more important now as the town contemplates its future. Concerns about Berwick's long-term economic performance and ageing demographic profile, coupled with the recognition that development pressures were intensifying, led to the inauguration in 2005 of a Berwick-upon-Tweed Masterplan, led by Berwick-upon-Tweed Borough Council with the support of the regional development agency One NorthEast, English Heritage and other regional and local partners. The Masterplan and subsequent Regeneration Stategy, now an integral part of a wider Berwick's Future initiative, sets out a vision for the town over the next 20 years and identifies where the principal opportunities lie. The wider initiative covers both physical regeneration and social improvements such as better access to education and skills opportunities. The Regeneration Strategy will be a complex undertaking. It will be more likely to yield solid, sustainable benefits if it is based on sound understanding of the historic environment – including the contribution that the latter can make not only to sense of place and quality of life, but to the economic well-being of the town.

This book presents something of the wealth of historic interest encapsulated in Berwick, Tweedmouth and Spittal, and explains how these places came to assume such varied and distinctive forms. Above all, it urges that a town anxious for stability and prosperity in the future should know where it has come from as well as where it is going.

Simon Thurley, Chief Executive of English Heritage

Councillor Isabel Hunter, Chair of Berwick's Future Partnership

1

Introduction: a border town on the borders of change

On 29 August 1850 a large crowd assembled to witness the formal opening, by Queen Victoria, of the Royal Border Bridge (Figs 1 and 2). In an age replete with great engineering feats, this was a momentous achievement – a magnificent railway viaduct striding high above the River Tweed and completing a permanent railway link between London and Edinburgh for the first time. Built by the York, Newcastle & Berwick Railway Co to replace an ungainly trestle bridge opened as a temporary measure two years earlier, the stone and brick viaduct rose 126ft 6in above the river bed on 28 semicircular arches.

The railway had reached Berwick a little earlier when the North British Railway Co opened its line between Edinburgh and Berwick in 1846. The following year the Newcastle & Berwick Railway Co (precursor of the York, Newcastle & Berwick) opened a temporary terminus on the opposite bank of the Tweed at Tweedmouth. In the 1840s the railway was the epitome of modernity and in its progress it was often careless of the past. The construction of Berwick Station entailed the demolition of substantial parts of Edward I's late 13th-century castle, which stood in the way (Fig 3). Despite being ruinous since the 16th century, the castle's thick masonry walls put up stiff resistance, compelling the navvies to resort to gunpowder to reduce them to rubble. The contractors – the Cumberland firm of Messrs McKay & Blackstock (James McKay and J Blackstock) – employed upwards of 2,000 men at the busiest period of the project, which required the construction of a series of coffer dams around each pier, the use of the new steam-powered piledriver invented in 1843 by Edinburgh-born James Nasmyth (1808–90) and the rearing of a huge embankment on the curved Tweedmouth approach. The work was superintended by the resident engineer George Barclay Bruce (1821–1908), under the general direction of one of the age's great industrial heroes, Robert Stephenson (1803–59), acting with the railway company's engineer-in-chief, Thomas Elliott Harrison (1808–88). It cost the then enormous sum of £184,143.[2]

More than 150 years later the engineering of the Royal Border Bridge continues to impress and for many rail travellers the vantage point which it affords provides their first impression of Berwick. Looking south-eastwards one sees the River Tweed – either broad and impressive or narrowly confined by shoals, depending on the state of the tide – pursuing its way to the North

Figure 1
The Royal Border Bridge, opened in 1850, symbolises Berwick's border location. Much of Berwick's ruined medieval castle was destroyed to make way for the railway.
[DP065297]

Figure 2
Salmon-fishing boats – called cobles – beached at the foot of Carlin Brae with the Royal Border Bridge beyond. This late 19th-century view is evocative of the contrasts between the traditional world and the new order ushered in by the railway and its viaduct.
[BB75/05723]

Sea through a narrow outlet nearly closed at low tide by a sand bar extending from Spittal Point. On each side lie substantial settlements: Berwick on the left rises steeply from the river's edge, the Town Hall steeple providing a notable accent; Tweedmouth on the right, much augmented by 20th-century residential and industrial estates, is separated by the Goody Patchy (a narrow belt of woodland and open ground) from Spittal, where a lone factory chimney on Spittal Point forms a memorable landmark. Two other bridges – the low, rugged, asymmetrically hump-backed, stone-arched Berwick Bridge of 1611–34 and Mouchel & Co's effortless ferroconcrete Royal Tweed Bridge (opened in 1928), leaping the river in just three rising and lengthening bounds (a fourth arch spans the low-lying ground on the Tweedmouth side) – are testament to the enduring importance of the Great North Road, whilst the occasional Russian freighter, nosing its way into Tweed Dock on the incoming tide, is a reminder of Berwick's longstanding trade connections with the Baltic and the North Sea.

In the opposite direction the view could hardly be more different. Far below the bridge parapet lies a fragment of the medieval defences, looking almost as though it had been pitched into the river by the all-conquering railway. Upstream the Tweed takes a broad sweep inland and its valley – for a while still steep on the Berwick side and gentler on the other – shows barely a trace of the town's proximity. An elegant early 19th-century out-of-town villa, Castle Hills House, catches the eye halfway up the steeper valley-side and below it the small white speck of Whitesands Shiel (until recently used by salmon fishermen) punctuates the curve of the river. But the sharpness of the contrast between town and country is misleading, for much of Berwick's wealth derived from the salmon fishery stretching far inland along the Tweed and from the produce of its rich agricultural hinterland.

Little is known of Berwick's earliest history. A Roman fort or settlement of some description on the Tweed, though as yet unverified, is highly likely and it was in any case natural that the developing regional network of roads should focus on Berwick and Tweedmouth. Though the Tweed is prone to violent floods – posing technological challenges which medieval bridge-builders struggled to overcome – the river was a considerable asset because it afforded one of the few natural harbours on the generally inhospitable coast between the Tyne and the Forth, while its great breadth rendered it shallow enough to be forded at low tide.

But if these natural advantages worked generally in Berwick's favour as a centre of trade and communications, the river's magnitude also made it a natural political frontier between the frequently warring kingdoms of England and Scotland. Since the more rugged northern bank was better adapted to fortification and blessed with the more sheltered (though not the deepest) anchorage, Berwick took the lead over its neighbours on the opposite bank. Once Scotland's richest royal burgh, Berwick was much prized both for its defensible position and for its lucrative wool trade – as a result it experienced a turbulent history. Edward I besieged and captured the town with much slaughter in 1296 and promptly set about building a new castle and other defences (Fig 4). By 1318 the Scots had regained their hold on Berwick, but their triumph was short-lived; the town was to change hands repeatedly before English rule was permanently established by Edward IV in 1482.

Figure 3
Today a fragment of Berwick Castle forms the disregarded backdrop to a track maintenance depot. [DP071134]

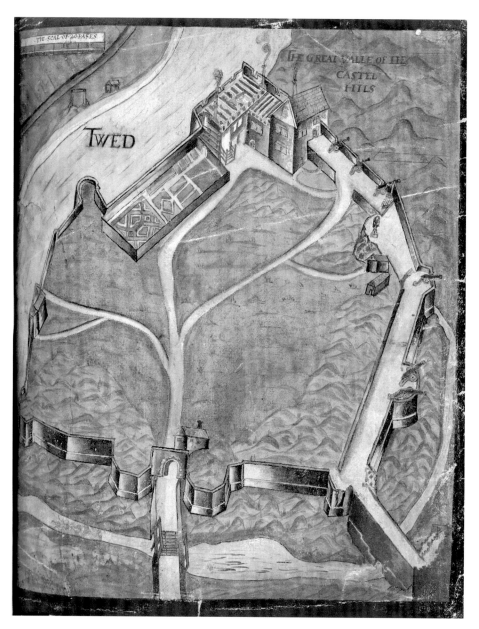

Figure 4
This late 16th-century plan of Berwick Castle captures its form just before it fell into disuse and decay. A mixture of stone and timber walls seems to be indicated, together with lead and tiled roofs and brick chimneys. An elaborate garden features prominently. At the bottom of the map the stream draining the Tappee Pond is crossed by a drawbridge.
[Bodleian Library, University of Oxford, Gough Gen Top. 374, vol 3, p256: View of Berwick Castle]

Following the English Reformation Henry VIII and Edward VI both made piecemeal alterations to the defences. However, it was not until the early years of Elizabeth's reign (1558–1603) that they were rebuilt in the manner of the latest Italian engineers – albeit on a reduced scale, abandoning roughly one-third of the area enclosed by the medieval walls (Fig 5). Lack of funds meant that elements of the medieval walls were retained along the river, but even so the topographer and antiquary William Camden (1551–1623) felt justified in describing Berwick as 'the last and best fortified town in all Britain'.[3] Tensions lessened after the union in 1603 of the English and Scottish crowns (when James VI of Scotland assumed the additional title of James I of England), though conflict was renewed on the eve of the Civil War and threatened again with the Jacobite rebellions of 1715 and 1745. Indeed in 1715 the fortification at Holy Island, maintained as an outpost of the Berwick garrison, was briefly captured in a daring Jacobite raid. By the end of the 18th century the Elizabethan ramparts were obsolete, but coastal defences were maintained against potential foreign aggressors until the end of the Second World War (*see* Fig 36) and Berwick's garrison did not finally vacate the Barracks until 1964.

Figure 5
Berwick's bastion defences. The introduction of the bastion system of defence revolutionised warfare in continental Europe, making its first appearance in late 15th-century Italy. Artillery sheltered behind the earthworks on top of the arrow-shaped bastions, and other guns swept the ground to either side, keeping an enemy from scaling or mining the ramparts.
[NMR 20688/13]

'Carlisle is the Key into England on the West as Berwick is on the East.'[4] So wrote a traveller in 1775, when the defences of both towns were still very much in commission, and the subsequent history of these two strongholds makes for an interesting comparison. Both were shaped by their border location, by their girdling walls and by the constant protection of a garrison. There was a price to pay, however, for the solicitude of the English crown, in the form of soldiers billeted on the local alehouses – a source of recurrent discontent in Berwick until the completion of the Barracks in 1721 relieved the townspeople of their burden. The walls, too, with their narrow and infrequent gates, resolutely barred at night, were an impediment to free movement and trade (*see* Fig 33). But there were compensations too. The garrison provided commercial opportunities for those who could provision them or supply other wants, and the town also benefited from the presence of high-ranking officers (including the crown-appointed governor), with their propensity to spend and their contribution, not uncommonly, to the wider cultural life of the town.

Berwick's peculiar border constitution (Fig 6), set out in the royal charter of 1604 and not rescinded (except briefly under James II) until 1835, shaped the development of the town in less obvious ways. Its political independence, vested in the Guild of Freemen, was highly prized but denied the town any role in the wider administration of either Northumberland or Berwickshire, while its largely self-sufficient judicial powers ruled it out as a location for the dispensing of justice at the county level. The resulting loss of office-holding opportunities was compounded by the fact that, unlike Carlisle, it was not the seat of a bishopric so it did not benefit from the wealth and patronage bestowed by those holding high church office. There was also less incentive for the rural landed elite, who might otherwise have treated Berwick as a natural social centre, to build town houses or to foster cultural institutions on the scale experienced in many other provincial towns. These economic disadvantages were compounded by geographical circumstances, which ensured that Berwick never became a major railway junction as Carlisle did. And when the railway arrived it undermined the town's coastal shipping while providing no compensating boost to its inland trade. The population figures for the two towns underline the contrast. In 1801 they were closely matched with Carlisle (including the out-townships) having 10,560 inhabitants and Berwick (including Tweedmouth and Spittal) numbering 11,146. But by 2001 Carlisle's

Figure 6
This extract from An Act for the Uniformity of Publick Prayers, *reprinted in the 1761 edition of the* Book of Common Prayer, *affirms the peculiar constitutional status enjoyed by Berwick for much of its history.* [Canon Alan Hughes, DP065716]

the alterations and additions, which have been ſo made and preſented to his Majeſty by the ſaid convocations, be the book, which ſhall be appointed to be uſed by all that officiate in all cathedral and collegiate churches and chapels, and in all chapels of colleges and halls in both the univerſities, and the colleges of *Eaton* and *Wincheſter*, and in all pariſh churches and chapels, within the kingdom of *England*, dominion of *Wales*, and town of *Berwick* upon *Tweed*, and by

Figure 7
Union or division? Berwick looks both north and south for emblems of its heritage and identity.
[DP071135]

population had increased nearly sevenfold to 71,753, while Berwick's, which reached 15,781 in 1851, had fallen back to 11,665.

Berwick's distinctive border heritage frequently prompts comment and finds expression in a variety of ways (Fig 7). After the Reformation England and Scotland developed somewhat different strands of Protestantism and, while the Church of England was a politically and socially powerful presence in Berwick, the bulk of the town's inhabitants adopted the tenets of the Church of Scotland (known in England as the Presbyterian church). This is reflected in the pattern of church and school building, which has more in common with Scottish towns than with their English counterparts. On the other hand, for those professional skills that are scarce in small towns Berwick looked as much to Newcastle upon Tyne (distant 64 miles) as to Edinburgh (54 miles). So in its buildings Berwick reflects the work of architects north and south of the border in addition to able and even talented local architects, such as the early 20th-century partnership of W Gray and George P Boyd. But in commerce, although both Edinburgh and Newcastle were significant trading partners, it is overwhelmingly the London trade that was the foundation of Berwick's prosperity.

It is in fact easy to overemphasise the significance of the border location. Berwick was always more than just a garrison town nervously alert to any renewal of hostilities. It was a market town and the foremost commercial centre between Newcastle and Edinburgh. Increasingly, from the 18th century, it acquired industrial muscle, albeit catering mainly for local consumption. As a fishing harbour it participated in the seasonal salmon and herring fisheries, while as a seaport it enjoyed a fluctuating share in the profitable coastwise trade (principally to London) in fish, agricultural produce and even coal, as well as the Scandinavian and Baltic trade in timber, hemp and iron. These activities forged links and led to patterns of development shared with a host of ports and havens all along the east coast of England and Scotland. Berwick's many crow-stepped gables, which are often invoked as proof of the town's Scottish character, can for example be paralleled in many places around the North Sea and Baltic littoral – an enclosed trading zone that functioned much like a northern version of the Mediterranean.

Tweedmouth and Spittal have received much less attention from historians and others than Berwick; their early history is poorly documented by comparison and they are all too easily overlooked by visitors. They shared in

Berwick's fortunes, good or ill, but they developed in markedly different ways. Free from the physical constraint of defensive walls, they formed part of a detached portion of County Durham called Islandshire and did not become part of Northumberland, nor fully under Berwick's jurisdiction, until 1835.

Tweedmouth and Spittal have always been less considerable settlements than Berwick but they were far from negligible. Tweedmouth Parish, which included Spittal, accounted for 32% of the total population of the three settlements in 1801,[5] rising to 38% by 1911.[6] Tweedmouth and Spittal have a more spacious layout than Berwick-within-the-ramparts, and the scale of building was, prior to the railway's arrival, generally smaller (Fig 8). These characteristics are shared with that portion of Berwick known as the Greenses, which became extramural in the 16th century and which evolved, like Tweedmouth and Spittal, almost as a separate village engaged principally in fishing and farming. With more space, fewer wealthy residents to offend, a pool of potential labour and, before their incorporation with Berwick, less stringent regulation of trades and industrial activities, Tweedmouth and Spittal were attractive to those wishing to set up large, noisy or polluting industrial enterprises; this tendency was accentuated in the 19th century as the scale of industrial activities grew and the developing railway and port infrastructure was concentrated on the Tweed's southern bank. In Spittal the fishing village acquired a distinct industrial quarter on the flat land of Spittal Point where a gasworks and several manure factories were among the less salubrious new arrivals. But barely more than a stone's throw away a small spa and sea-bathing resort flourished, taking advantage of a chalybeate spring and a nearby sandy beach (Fig 9). More recently, Tweedmouth and Spittal absorbed much of Berwick's physical expansion as overcrowding within the walls was relieved by the building of housing estates, many of them on the south side of the Tweed.

Competing interests and fluctuating fortunes will continue to influence the future of Berwick, Tweedmouth and Spittal. The aspirations of long-term residents, retired incomers, second-home owners, visitors, business leaders, council planners and others will frequently not coincide and may sometimes conflict with one another. In recent years there has been much discussion about Berwick's future and opinions have sometimes been sharply divided over the extent to which development should be encouraged as a way of delivering

Figure 8
Tweedmouth has the population of a small town but it retains many characteristics from its village origins, giving it a small-scale, intimate feel. This open court off Main Street remains much as it was in 1943 when L S Lowry painted it.
[DP065275]

Figure 9
Spittal originated as a fishing village, but during the 19th and early 20th centuries a small seaside resort coexisted uneasily with an area of concentrated industrial development, memorialised by the distant chimney.
[DP065266]

economic prosperity and social stability. The interests of the future and the legacy of the past are sometimes seen as diametrically opposed to one another, though they need not be so. The past is both a creative stimulus and a vital ingredient in the quality of individual lives. This book sets out to explain how the varied landscapes, buildings, streets and open spaces of Berwick, Tweedmouth and Spittal assumed their present form and to celebrate the resulting variety that the town presents to residents and visitors alike.

2

A town takes shape

The personality of a town is the distillation of a wide range of physical and cultural influences. One of the most important of these is the underlying landscape. Towns, especially in their early development, respond intimately to features in the landscape that may now be all but invisible. And their distinctive character is reinforced by the prevalence of particular building materials, which in turn reflect local geology. This chapter explores the influence of natural landforms – and the natural resources that they yielded – on the origin, evolution and appearance of Berwick, Tweedmouth and Spittal.

The landscape beneath

Standing on the Tweedmouth side of the Tweed near Berwick Bridge, and imagining that Berwick is not there, one can visualise the promontory on which the town is built dipping gradually south-eastwards towards the sea, where it terminates in low, poorly consolidated cliffs. These cliffs increase in height northwards from the river's mouth, giving a more dramatic feel to the cove known as Greenses Haven, and continue in the direction of the rocky foreland of St Abb's Head, some 13 miles distant. The town (Fig 10) is mostly built on the gently sloping south-western flank of the promontory, which terminates (most abruptly in West Street and Eastern Lane) at a steep escarpment plunging towards the riverside. Those parts of the escarpment that are not built up are still known locally as 'braes' or 'banks'. West of the town, near Carlin Brae (Fig 11), the fall to the river from Castle Terrace is as much as 50m; by the time we reach the eastern ramparts it is no more than 10m, and further east the brae merges with the low sea cliff. The only appreciable area of flat land is the Ness (east of Sandgate and south of Ness Street), which juts out from the Berwick shore at the point where the low-water channel seeks the Spittal bank. The town's quay grew up north-west of the Ness, between Bridge Street and Quay Walls, at the point where the river scours the Berwick shore but is sheltered from storms by the Ness. However, from an early date Berwick's principal streets extended on to the higher ground.

There are braes on the opposite side of the Tweed as well and, because the land here is less built up than in central Berwick, they are even more apparent

Figure 10
Berwick from the air. The compactness of the town and the scarcity of large open spaces are immediately apparent.
[NMR 20687/55]

to the eye. Spittal and part of Tweedmouth originated at their foot, safe from the violence of river and sea but close enough to make the most of the fishing they afforded, and each settlement has a back lane (that in Tweedmouth known as Yard Heads) running along the top of the brae, separating the house plots from the fields above. Tweedmouth's origins can probably be traced to a tight knot of streets around St Bartholomew's Church (Fig 12), where passengers fording the river from Berwick made their landfall. However, from an early date there were other elements to the settlement: a polyfocal pattern emerged as crossing points changed and Tweedmouth was pulled this way and that. One of the early bridges planted the seeds of the bridgehead and thoroughfare suburb which grew up along the realigned Great North Road, and may also have prompted the emergence of a small fishermen's settlement around a green at West End.

Spittal is set apart from the main road, lying, like much of Tweedmouth, practically on the foreshore at the foot of Spittal Banks, so-called on a map of 1837 (*see* the map of Spittal on the inside back cover). Dock Road now links

Figure 11
Natural topography exerted a decisive influence on the development of Berwick and was exploited for defensive purposes. At Carlin Brae, adjoining the castle, the natural river terrace falls sharply to the flat riverside. In the 19th century the crest of the escarpment was exploited for the building of villas along what became known as Castle Terrace.
[DP065219]

Figure 12
Brewery Bank forms part of the irregular cluster of narrow streets surrounding St Bartholomew's Church and forming the nucleus of the medieval village.
[DP065282]

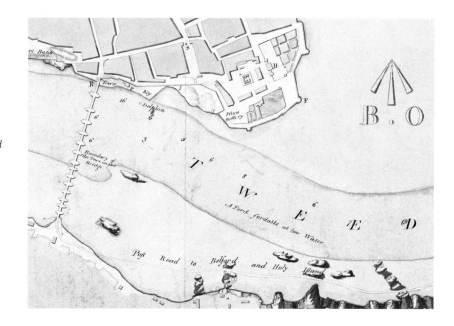

Figure 13
Key features of early communications emerge from this map of Berwick. It is an 1808 copy of a 1747 map reproducing, with revisions, a map that was first prepared in 1725. The ford across the Tweed is indicated as is the course of the main road south, preferring the hard sands of the foreshore to the elevated overland route. Eventually this route became Dock Road. [The National Archives, MPH 1/228/1]

the two settlements, but in earlier centuries traffic passed directly along the sands (Fig 13) and it is likely that Spittal's wide Main Street (formerly Front Street) was originally built up only on the landward side like Tweedmouth's Main Street. Between Middle Street, which runs along the rear of the Main Street plots, and West Street there is an area of infill that may have been a green originally. Part of the ecclesiastical parish of Tweedmouth until 1871, Spittal (a variant of the Middle English word for hospital) took its name from the long-vanished medieval hospital of St Bartholomew, which also gave the name to a farmhouse, Spittal Hall Farm, demolished in the 20th century for housing. Spittal was once home principally to fishermen and colliers working small pits on the higher ground of Tweedmouth Moor. North and South Greenwich Roads bear witness to the fact that much of Spittal belonged to Greenwich Hospital – the great seamen's hospital on the Thames – which had acquired the estates of the 3rd Earl of Derwentwater, executed for his role in the 1715 Jacobite Rising.

The modern visitor to Berwick may wonder where the townspeople derived water for domestic and industrial uses before the advent of a modern piped supply. The Tweed is tidal four miles inland as far as Union Bridge near Horncliffe and therefore it is unsuitable for drinking and many other purposes. Nowhere else in modern Berwick, Tweedmouth and Spittal is surface water apparent. Berwick in particular must have always depended heavily on wells. Its wealthier citizens would have had wells of their own (one, in the yard of a house on Wallace Green, was considered by the Ordnance Survey to be an antiquity in the 1850s), but for the rest there were public wells. Many of them, if not all, remained in use long enough to be recorded by the surveyors of the 1852 Board of Health map and the majority have names which attest to long familiarity. A number had medicinal qualities attributed to them. The Cat Well, which was located at the bottom of Hide Hill at its junction with Silver Street, was described in 1799 as 'much resorted to by people with tender eyes; and … has been found useful in scorbutic and stomach complaints', whilst the Spa Well – so popular by 1799 that 'in the summer season, many who have come to drink it have been obliged to go home again for want of lodgings'[7] – was the reason for Spittal's emergence as a minor spa and sea-bathing resort (*see* Fig 93).

The wells were supplemented by public 'pants' or fountains located in a number of major streets – one in Castlegate where it broadens out at the site of the former cattle market next to the present St Mary's Church, one at the top of Hide Hill (Fig 14) and another nearby at the top of Sandgate. By the 16th century water was being supplied via a conduit from Pettekar Lough, created by damming a small stream near New East Farm, close to the Scottish border. The absence of a reservoir in Berwick itself made the provision of water uncertain in times of drought; water was also depleted by better-off residents who paid to divert it from the public supply via small pipes known as 'sprigs'.[8] These problems may explain why water for the Governor's House arrived via lead pipes laid across the river bed from St Cuthbert's Well in Tweedmouth.[9] Towards the end of the 18th century an additional water source was brought into use at New Close, a mile west of Berwick near Letham Shank, and the combined supply was collected in a new covered reservoir at the foot of Castlegate, just outside the Scotch Gate.

Contrary to modern appearances, each settlement had in fact at least one small stream capable of being dammed so as to accumulate enough water to drive machinery. In Berwick one stream descended the deeply incised valley (Castle Vale), which medieval engineers incorporated into the south-eastward defences of the castle. It was penned at Castle Bridge (also known as Castlegate Bridge) to form the Tappee Pond. In the medieval period it powered a mill immediately below the bridge, but by the early 18th century it powered two watermills – High Mill next to the bridge and Low Mill nearer the Tweed

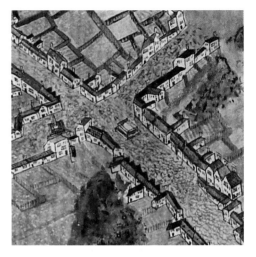

Figure 14
The 'pant' or public well (centre) at the top of Hide Hill, as shown in a detail from the 'True Description' of c 1580. *The medieval market cross can be seen to the left on the site of the present Town Hall. For a larger extract from this map, see* Fig 28.
[British Library Board, All Rights Reserved, Cotton Augustus I, II, f.14]

Figure 15
High Mill and Low Mill harnessed the waters of the
diminutive stream tumbling down the ravine between the
castle and Tweed Street. They were supplemented in the
18th century by a windmill within the walls of the ruined
castle. This map, made in 1839, depicts the planned
course of the railway that would destroy all three mills
within ten years.
[Berwick-upon-Tweed Record Office, T1/2]

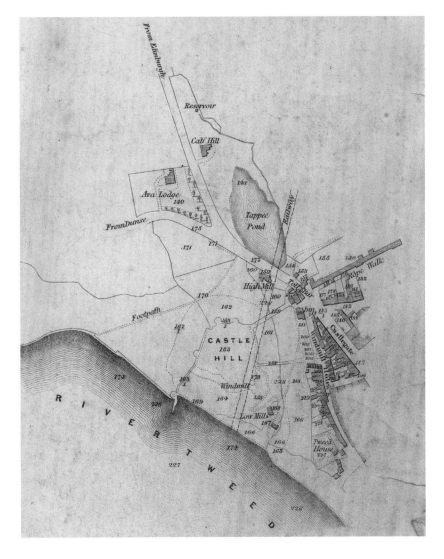

(Fig 15). These disappeared in the mid-1840s when the North British Railway Co built Berwick Station, infilling the pond to create level ground for its goods yard and locomotive shed; however, the suitability of their sites for water power can still be appreciated in the municipal gardens below the station approach, while a vestige of the Tappee Pond is now a wetland Site of Natural Conservation Importance.

On the other side of the river a handful of tiny streams emerged from a spring-line in the steep slope bordering the flood plain. In Tweedmouth the course of one stream is indicated by the short sloping street known as Mill Strand; it seems to have been sufficient to power both a corn mill (latterly the Tweed Flour Mill or Short's Mill), part of which survives on Dock Road, and later the Border Brewery, which stands higher up on Brewery Bank. Further south-east another stream accounts for the steep incision still bridged by the short viaduct of the Tweed Dock Branch Railway. Both streams have watermills shown alongside them on the *c* 1580 'True Description' map (*see* Fig 28), which also depicts the mill next to Castle Bridge.[10] In Spittal, Fuller noted in 1799 that at Davidson's blue mill ('blue', in the form of cake or powder, was used for laundering clothes) a 'spring of water runs through the premises [sic] sufficient to drive machinery of considerable extent'[11] (Fig 16). As late as 1852 this stream, by then powering a small corn mill, still passed along a substantial stretch of Main Street in an open channel, but nowadays this and the other streams are all culverted.

Where water power was unavailable or inadequate, wind power might be an option. Windmills necessarily adopted exposed, usually elevated, situations. None is shown on the Bucks' 1740s view of the town (*see* Fig 35a); however, by the end of the 18th century one had been erected within the ruins of the castle, where it appears in a view by C Catton Jnr and F Jukes published in 1793 (*see* Fig 49); either this or another nearby must have given the name of Windmill Hole to what is now Tweed Street. Other early windmills stood on or near the ramparts overlooking Magdalene Fields – one gave its name to the Windmill Bastion and another stood on the site of Lions House. Wind power, of course, was also the mainstay of Berwick's seaborne trade before steamships became a viable alternative in the second quarter of the 19th century.

Figure 16 (above)
The recently fire-damaged Spittal mill worked as a blue mill as well as a corn mill.
[DP065632]

The Liberty of Berwick

Berwick was generously supplied with agricultural land on the north bank of the Tweed, extending some three miles north of the walled town almost to the Scottish village of Lamberton and a similar distance westwards, including the hamlets of Gainslaw and High and Low Cocklaw. This sparsely inhabited country, known as Berwick Bounds or the Liberty of Berwick (Fig 17), was

Figure 17 (right)
Berwick was endowed with lands north of the Tweed known as the Liberty of Berwick, which supplied agricultural produce, mineral resources and industrial sites. In 1657 the manors of Tweedmouth and Spittal, with attendant mineral rights, were acquired and in 1835 the townships of Tweedmouth and Spittal were absorbed within the borough.

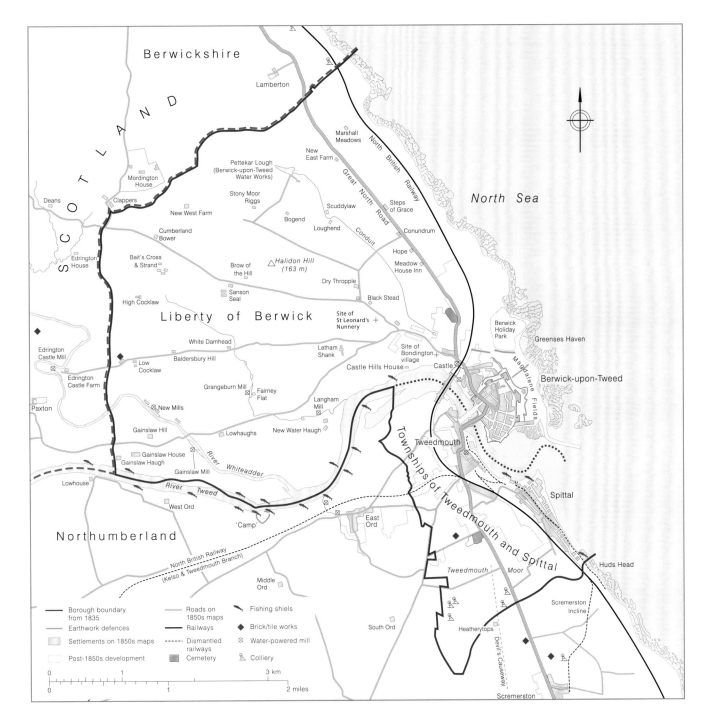

Berwickshire

Lamberton

S C O T L A N D

Deans

Mordington House

Clappers

New West Farm

Cumberland Bower

Bait's Cross & Strand

Edrington House

High Cocklaw

Edrington Castle Mill

Edrington Castle Farm

Paxton

Low Cocklaw

New Mills

Gainslaw Hill

Gainslaw House

Gainslaw Haugh

Gainslaw Mill

Lowhouse

West Ord

'Camp'

Northumberland

North British Railway (Kelso & Tweedmouth Branch)

Middle Ord

South Ord

East Ord

New East Farm

Marshall Meadows

Pettekar Lough (Berwick-upon-Tweed Water Works)

Stony Moor Riggs

Bogend

Brow of the Hill

Sanson Seal

White Damhead

Baldersbury Hill

Grangeburn Mill

Fairney Flat

Langham Mill

Lowhaughs

New Water Haugh

Scuddylaw

Loughend

△ Halidon Hill (163 m)

Dry Thropple

Liberty of Berwick

Site of St Leonard's Nunnery

Letham Shank

Castle Hills House

River Whiteadder

River Tweed

Steps of Grace

Conundrum

Conduit

Hope

Meadow House Inn

Black Stead

Site of Bondington village

Castle

North British Railway

Great North Road

North Sea

Berwick Holiday Park

Greenses Haven

Magdalene Fields

Berwick-upon-Tweed

Tweedmouth

Spittal

Townships of Tweedmouth and Spittal

Tweedmouth Moor

Heatherytops

Devil's Causeway

Huds Head

Scremerston Incline

Scremerston

— Borough boundary from 1835	—— Roads on 1850s maps
— Earthwork defences	— Railways
▨ Settlements on 1850s maps	--- Dismantled railways
☐ Post-1850s development	▨ Cemetery

Fishing shiels

◆ Brick/tile works

⊗ Water-powered mill

⚒ Colliery

0   1   3 km

0   1   2 miles

Figure 18
One of Tweedmouth's farmsteads, its yard full of ricks,
can be seen in the lower left-hand corner of this view
of Tweedmouth and Berwick taken on 3 October 1932.
To the right Short's Mill and the Border Brewery are
clearly shown.
[AFL03/Aerofilms/40678]

granted to the freemen and confirmed in James I's charter of 1604. Inland from the Liberty, on both sides of the Tweed, lay an extensive agricultural hinterland.

The Liberty was managed for the benefit of the freemen, both individually and collectively. The better land was leased – as were watermills, quarries and other industrial sites – supplementing the corporation's income from wharfage and tolls. In the late 18th and early 19th centuries there were corn mills at Gainslaw, New Mills and Grangeburn, and another at New Water Haugh, where there was also a snuff mill. Freemen could lease land on their own behalf and were entitled to stints (rights to pasture animals) on the commons. Many engaged in farming on a greater or lesser scale, a few centring their activities in the Liberty, but most treating agriculture as subsidiary to a trade, and some perhaps exercising their rights only to the extent of pasturing a cow on the Magdalene Fields to ensure a constant supply of fresh milk. On the fringes of Berwick the 1852 Board of Health map shows numerous barns, some equipped with horse-driven threshing engines. In the less densely built-up Greenses, numerous closes and paddocks survived into the 19th century and the Bull Well was doubtless once used to water cattle.

Tweedmouth and Spittal also had their farmsteads, where corn was gathered and stored in ricks prior to threshing (Fig 18). In Tweedmouth, on the present Main Street, there was a pinfold for collecting strayed livestock and in Spittal the Cow Road ascended the brae slantwise to reach the common pasture of Tweedmouth Moor. For centuries nearly two-thirds of the land in Tweedmouth Parish was common land managed through a system of stints rather than ownership and formal division. By the late 18th century educated opinion had moved decisively against the system of commons, which were seen as a hindrance to innovation and efficiency, as well as a harbour for disorderly social elements, and in 1800 Tweedmouth Moor was enclosed. A similar process transformed the commons within the Liberty.

Many of Berwick's industries processed agricultural produce or by-products. Cereals were milled for both human and animal consumption – much was stockpiled in huge granaries prior to shipping and some barley was destined for malting and brewing – while the by-products of arable farming included straw for thatch and hat-making. Livestock yielded hides for tanning and shoe-making, and tallow for soap-making and cheap candles, as well as horn and bonemeal. Wool and flax supplied the textile industry. In the late

18th century kelp (a type of seaweed rich in iodine) was gathered on the beach beneath the Magdalene Fields, burnt to produce potash and either used as a fertiliser or sold to glass and soap-makers further afield. The surrounding landscape is not abundantly wooded and, in all likelihood, has not been for centuries. Fortunately the great pine forests of Scandinavia and the Baltic were within reach and Berwick's buildings, in common with those of most east coast ports, make early use of imported softwoods.

Fruits of the earth

Berwick also enjoyed a range of mineral resources. The great Northumberland and Durham coalfield, which has scarred the land and dramatically shaped the economic development of the North-East, may seem a world away from Berwick's small-town charm, but local people recall that as late as the 1950s there was a working pit immediately to the south. Berwick Corporation purchased the Lordships of the Manors of Tweedmouth and Spittal in 1657 primarily to bring the wharfage and shipping on the Tweed (with the power to levy valuable tolls) entirely under its control, though it acquired mineral rights to the land at the same time. These yielded coal – known locally as 'culm' – and for many years the town had its own colliery at Sunnyside, south of Tweedmouth. There was another at Berwick Hill on Tweedmouth Moor and further collieries operated in the neighbourhood of Scremerston. Together these small pits helped to defray the costs of importing coal from the Tyne and also generated a small coastal trade.

The rugged sandstone from which most of the town is built comes largely from the area immediately south of Tweedmouth and Spittal (Fig 19). The stone was plentiful and quarries grew up in favourable locations, often next to roads or by the sea for ease of transportation. Berwick Bridge is said to have been built using stone from a quarry in Tweedmouth, immediately behind the site later occupied by the Tower Foundry. The very large King's Quarry at Sunnyside was later adapted as the site of Tweedmouth Cemetery (opened 1858). Sources further afield might be used for the best quality stone. Stone for the western half of the Town Hall was quarried at Edrington Castle,

Figure 19
The sandstone used in Berwick, Tweedmouth and Spittal ranges from brown to pink. Few houses employ it so strikingly as Eagle House (48 Tweed Street and 11 Railway Street), the work of William Wilson, monumental mason and sculptor of Tweedmouth. [DP065712]

Berwickshire, but the corporation's own quarry at New Mills, within the Liberty, was used when the eastern half was built, perhaps to reduce the expense.[12] Limestone outcropped in the low cliffs sheltering Fishermen's Haven and Greenses Haven north of Berwick (Fig 20), where in the 18th century there were a series of limekilns. The polished black whinstone setts that pave a number of lesser streets and courts in Berwick, including Dewar's Lane and Oil Mill Lane, may have been quarried at Embleton (Fig 21).

Buildings faced in brick were relatively rare in Berwick before the 20th century (the former vicarage on the Parade and the house known as The Retreat on The Avenue (Fig 22) are among the exceptions), but from the early 18th century onwards most houses used brick for internal walls and chimneys. The Barracks, though faced in stone, is built predominantly of brick produced at Tweedmouth. Pantiles are recorded as incoming cargo from the Netherlands

Figure 20 (below, left)
The striking shelf in the cliff above Greenses Haven (indicated by the shorter grass) results from large-scale limestone quarrying in the 18th century.
[DP065623]

Figure 21 (below, right)
Dewar's Lane, off Bridge Street, is one of a number of minor roads and yards still paved with whinstone setts. The tall building on the right, its wall leaning and distorted, is the mid-18th-century former granary of Dewar & Carmichael, corn and iron merchants. Empty for more than 20 years, it is being converted to a youth hostel, cafe and exhibition space.
[DP056360]

in the early 18th century and by the end of the century they were being manufactured locally, rapidly supplanting thatch and giving the town its characteristically warm roofscapes. Less conspicuous than the red pantiles – and now a good deal rarer – are the roofs of 'Scotch slates' (Fig 23). With their small size and rough texture these blackish slates contrast with the Welsh and Cumbrian slates that supplanted them after the middle of the 19th century.

Figure 22
The Retreat, a brick house on The Avenue, dates from the second half of the 18th century. Red brick appears relatively infrequently in Berwick, though some brick houses are thinly disguised with paint.
[DP065249]

Figure 23
Roofs are prominent in views across the Tweed and in all but the narrowest streets. The roof on the left has Scotch slates; the roof on the right and in the left foreground has Welsh slates; and beyond clay pantiles.
[DP071136]

Communications

There has probably been a river crossing at Berwick since at least Roman times. The Roman road known further south as the Devil's Causeway follows an alignment that, if projected northwards, suggests that the river was bridged or forded just below St Bartholomew's Church. As late as 1799 Fuller noted: 'That part of the river opposite the ballast key is called the Ford, from stones usually collected there by floods. Owing to those stones and other rubbish the river is shallower here than in any other part of it below the bridge'[13] – doubtless this was the route used by medieval travellers during those long intervals in which Berwick lacked a bridge. Pursuing the route northwards there is a pronounced alignment of streets in Berwick itself – Sandgate, Hide Hill, then, via a slight sidestep, Church Street, Wallace Green and, outside the 16th-century ramparts, Low Greens. The proximity of Holy Trinity Church (the present 17th-century building replaces a medieval precursor) argues for the antiquity of the route. Mid-19th-century maps of Berwick show a footpath continuing the line of Low Greens across the ramparts (where documents record the existence of a gate early in the history of the medieval defences) to a junction with the Great North Road, which now turns aside abruptly on its southward course to enter Berwick via Castlegate. The diversion is likely to have followed the establishment either of Edward I's castle or its Scottish forerunner.

Castlegate and its continuation, Marygate, are also of considerable antiquity. They form part of the road to Edrington Castle and the Berwickshire town of Duns, a route which, as Castle Terrace, passes the site of the deserted medieval village of Bondington. The effect of the castle, therefore, was to magnify the importance of these roads at the expense of part of the old north–south route. Further modifications to the street pattern were associated with successive bridges over the Tweed, which gave their name to Bridge Street. Once again, the street probably already existed before the bridge confirmed its importance. The first bridge whose existence is firmly documented existed in the reign of Malcolm IV of Scotland (1153–65), but was destroyed by a flood in 1199. Two bridges followed one after another in the 13th century, but when the second was destroyed by a flood in 1294, Berwick was left bridgeless for some two centuries. The positions of these early bridges are not known, but it is likely

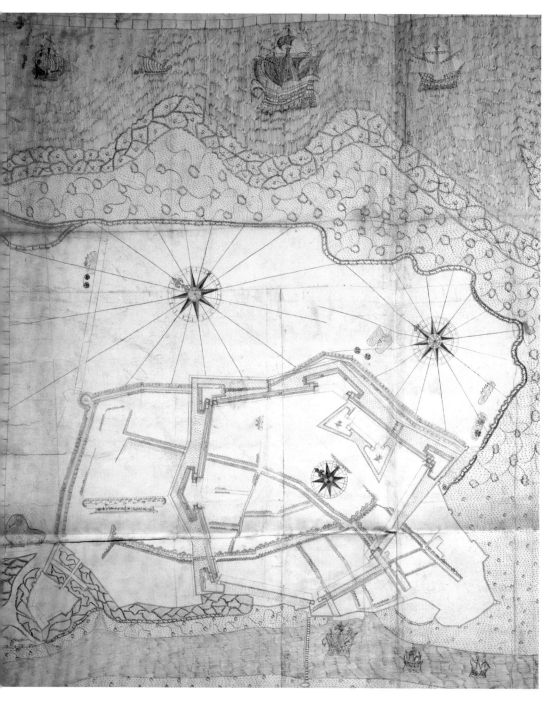

Figure 24
Berwick's last medieval bridge, built in the late 15th century, is shown here on a manuscript map prepared c 1561 by Rowland Johnson. Whereas the present bridge continues the alignment of West Street, its precursor left the Berwick shore further north at the end of what is now Love Lane.
[By kind permission of the Marquess of Salisbury, Hatfield House, Hatfield Maps CPM I. 22]

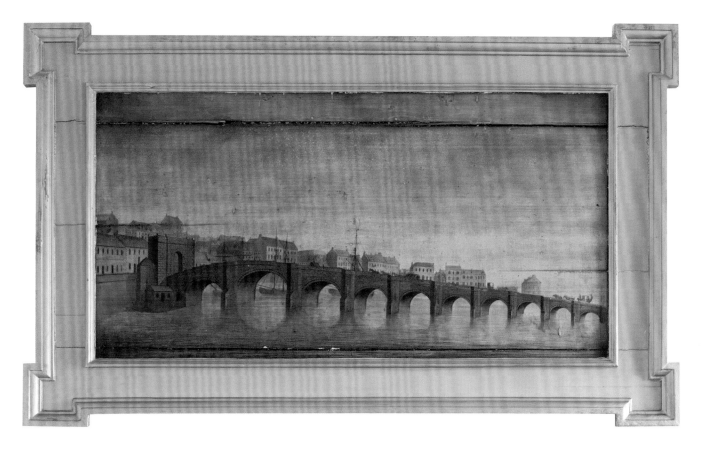

Figure 25
Berwick Bridge, as depicted by an anonymous artist in an oil painting on panelling in one of the bedrooms of the King's Arms Hotel. Although the panelling dates from the mid-18th century, the painting is later – its careful depiction of architectural details allows it to be dated quite precisely. It shows the first two houses of *Wellington Row, which were newly built in 1816, as well as the English Gate (or Bridge Gate), which was demolished in 1825.*
[DP065726]

that they were not far distant from the present stone bridge. A new wooden bridge was built in the late 15th century, probably by Henry VII, and appears on a number of maps, including one by Rowland Johnson preserved at Hatfield House (Fig 24). It crossed the river a little to the north of the present bridge, commencing at the northern end of Love Lane, and probably touching the Tweedmouth shore at the point where Main Street and West End meet. Love Lane was then the northern extremity of a line of streets – Bridge Street, Silver Street and Ness Street – which may all once have overlooked the foreshore like the Main Streets of Tweedmouth and Spittal. The present well-documented Berwick Bridge (Fig 25) – lengthy extracts from the building accounts were published by Fuller in 1799 – replaced that shown by Johnson; its prolonged construction – between 1611 and 1634 – was interrupted by floods. Once it was built the northern tip of Bridge Street dwindled in importance (Love Lane hints at a disreputable later history) and when its seaward side was built up some time after about 1580 its width was encroached upon.

The existence of other streets, sometimes with long-forgotten names, is confirmed by medieval documents. Briggate is recognisably the forerunner of Bridge Street, modern Church Street occurs as Soutergate (street of the shoemakers), Palace Street's humble origins are betrayed by its medieval name of Fishergate and Hide Hill first appears in the records as Uddinggate. The Greenses, a substantial area lying within the medieval walls to the east of Castlegate, seem never to have been heavily built up; indeed their name suggests that they functioned primarily as areas of pasture for livestock belonging to townsfolk. This probably explains why Elizabeth I's engineer could leave them outside the new ramparts, creating what a late 17th-century French visitor called 'an upper and a lower town'.[14] The impact of the new defences is still striking today. When one looks along Wallace Green, an unusually broad street now lined with mostly three-storeyed buildings, the view is abruptly terminated by the huge earthen bank of the rampart (Fig 26). Beyond the moat on the other side, the narrow lane called Low Greens is lined with small one- and two-storeyed buildings. The sharp contrast between the two streets reflects the separate development – prolonged over more than 400 years – of what was once a single thoroughfare.

The buildings of the early town

What kind of town took shape amid this landscape? Today Berwick, Tweedmouth and Spittal are composed predominantly of 18th- and 19th-century buildings, with 20th-century developments dominating the peripheries. With the exception of its fragmentary castle and medieval walls, Berwick has few outward traces of its earlier importance and many details of its medieval topography remain tantalisingly obscure. Its importance is attested by its status as a Scottish royal burgh and by the largest concentration of religious foundations between Newcastle and Edinburgh.

Figure 26
The abrupt termination of a street as broad as Wallace Green seems incongruous and results from the superimposition of Elizabethan defences on a medieval street pattern. Beyond the rampart the line of Wallace Green is continued by a much narrower lane called Low Greens.
[NMR 20386/15]

Figure 27
Berwick's only known wallpainting – an 'antiquework'
scheme from the former Old Hen & Chickens Inn on
Bridge Street – dates from the late 16th century. The
most complete scheme of its type in Northumberland,
it suggests a town far from isolated from the leading
trends and fashions of the day.
[Berwick-upon-Tweed Museum & Art Gallery,
DP065722]

Only a comprehensive inspection of the town's building stock will determine how much survives from the 17th century or earlier, disguised by later rebuilding. It is likely that the better buildings were built of stone but that lesser buildings, including many houses, were timber-framed; however, even within this broad framework there are likely to have been wide variations, with houses in the more densely built-up core of the town assuming forms quite different from those in the outlying settlements and areas. Early-looking houses are not numerous and their small number renders generalisations dangerous. But chance finds have illustrated the potential for survival in the town's historic core. Around 1900 a late 16th-century wallpainting scheme was uncovered in the Old Bridge Tavern (formerly the Old Hen & Chickens) on Bridge Street. The building was demolished in the 1960s to open up access to the public car park behind Bridge Street, but the wallpainting was removed and conserved, and is now exhibited at Berwick-upon-Tweed Museum & Art Gallery (Fig 27). The monochrome design is a parade of Renaissance details and a reminder that Berwick, through its coastal and overseas trade, was in touch with wider currents of taste and learning. The design also incorporates a proverb or motto – 'Wysedome & science, whiche are pure by kynde, / Shulde not be wryt in bookes, but in mynde,' – which the artist has placed on a panel depicted as though it is being turned, like a roasting spit, by an angel with outspread wings. It is not known whether the Old Hen & Chickens was originally an inn, though it

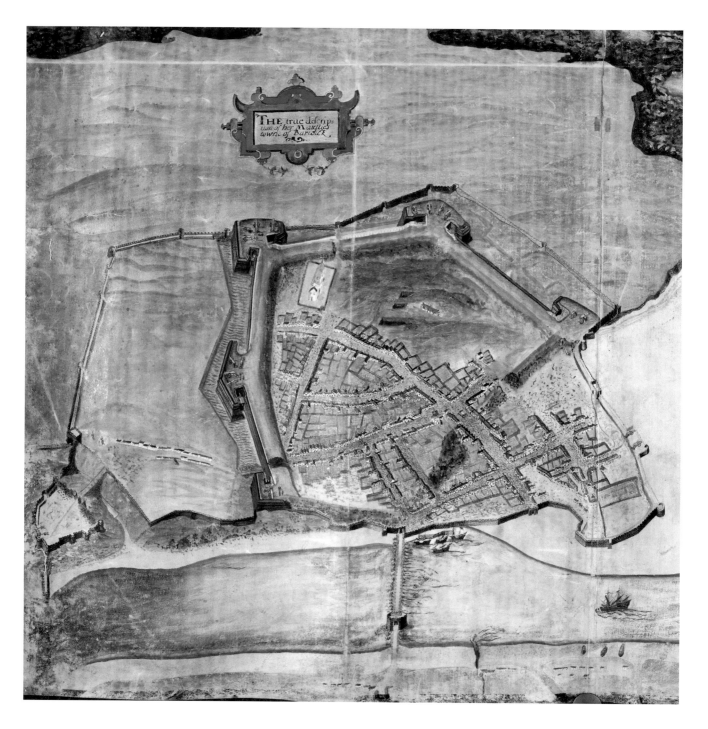

THE true descrip
tion of her Maiesties
towne of Barwick.

28

Figure 28 (left)
This bird's-eye view, entitled 'The true description of her Majesties towne of Barwick', was made c 1580 and although its main purpose was probably to document the recent fortifications and plan for the defence of the town, it also contains a wealth of architectural and other detail.
[British Library Board, All Rights Reserved, Cotton Augustus I, II, f.14]

Figure 29 (below)
This chest, now in Holy Trinity Church, incorporates panels thought to have been retrieved from the Earl of Dunbar's house built within the castle in the early years of the 17th century.
[DP065615]

may have been; perhaps it was the house of a wealthy merchant, who may have had a warehouse to the rear enjoying easy access to the town wharf.

While physical evidence for the early town remains in short supply, there are other sources to which we can turn for illumination. Berwick's strategic importance meant that it was mapped earlier and in more detail than most English towns. The best of these early maps, now in the British Library, dates from about 1580 and depicts the town not far removed from its medieval form (Fig 28; *see also* Fig 14). It is an astonishingly detailed piece of cartography, cast in the form of a bird's-eye view, and if it would be rash to credit every detail as correct, there is enough careful differentiation of buildings and other features to suggest that at least the more important among them are depicted with a degree of specificity. Roof materials are differentiated by different colours. The commonest is brown, which would appear to be thatch, still to be seen on roofs in Marygate according to a traveller's account of 1704.[15] But there are also small numbers of red and grey roofs, which must indicate tiles on the one hand and either lead or slate on the other (the main roof of Holy Trinity Church is grey, and the grey roofs correlate with taller or more prestigious buildings). One isolated building to the east of Church Street is clearly shown with a decorative timber-framed upper storey. The pant or fountain at the top of Hide Hill and a market cross on the site of the present Town Hall are shown, while a raw brown scar of uncultivated, unenclosed ground stretching from the foot of West Street almost to the King's Mount shows both the prominence of the brae in the town's topography and also its defensive potential – in 1562 work was under way building the defensive Cat Wall (or Cat Well Wall) along the course of the brae.[16]

Of Berwick's greatest 17th-century building – the lavish house built within the castle by the Earl of Dunbar from 1605 – only fragments survive (Fig 29). But a small number of lesser buildings of similar date can be identified in modern Berwick. A house with crow-stepped gables – 41 and 43 Bridge Street – has a late 16th- or early 17th-century stone fireplace. At 2 Shoe Lane, a small yard and alley linking Bridge Street with Eastern Lane, there is a two-storeyed building of plastered timber construction with a steeply pitched pantiled roof and a shallow jetty or projection to the upper floor (Fig 30). It is notable that the plain joists supporting the upper floor are of softwood and of widely varying cross-section, suggesting that this was a building of low status, possibly a warehouse. Another timber frame almost certainly lies concealed behind the

Figure 30 (far left)
2 Shoe Lane is one of just a handful of
identified timber-framed buildings in Berwick.
The hipped bay at the left end is an addition,
also in timber. The tall building beyond is the
Maltings Arts Centre, a former granary.
[DP065193]

Figure 31 (left)
Thin walls and a pattern of cracks in the
plaster – inconsistent with a masonry structure
– suggest that this bakery standing at the top of
Hide Hill is also timber-framed.
[DP065144]

plastered front of James Ford & Son's bakery at the top of Hide Hill (Fig 31). In West End, Tweedmouth, The Thatch public house preserves the walls of a stone house, probably of the 17th century; the distinctively off-centre entrance indicates a traditional cross-passage plan in which front and rear entrances faced each other at one end of the main living room of the house. Prior to a serious fire in 1886 the building was thatched and there was a cross-wing on the north side of the cross-passage; the cross-wing gable facing the street was dismantled during the rebuilding but a steeply pitched stone gable is still visible to the rear, though the covering is now of slate. At the time of the fire, The Thatch was described as 'perhaps the only thatched house then remaining in the borough'.[17] Pantiles and slate were by then practically universal.

Many of the houses in Berwick, Tweedmouth and Spittal would have been much more cramped and ill-built than The Thatch. The 'True Description' (*see* Fig 28) shows numbers of small, irregularly built houses in the Fishergate (now Palace Street and Foul Ford) area of the Ness and a number of other places. Inequalities in wealth and material conditions emerge from the records of the Hearth Tax in the third quarter of the 17th century. These indicate that the average number of taxable hearths per household in Berwick (2.48) exceeded that of Newcastle (2.06) though it was lower than that of York (3.2).[18] In Berwick's wealthiest area, in and around Bridge Street, the average rose to 3.3 per household, but in the poorest area, centred on Palace Street, it was a mere 1.7 hearths. Here a sizeable proportion of the houses clearly had just a single hearth; as the area became more fashionable in the 18th century these houses were swept away.

3

Political, social and spiritual order

Secular authority in Berwick derived from two main sources: the crown, in the person of the governor, backed up by the presence of a garrison, and the corporation through its mayor and other elected officers and, until the 1830s, the freemen or burgesses who elected both them and the town's two MPs. The crown was responsible for the defence of the realm against external aggressors and domestic insurrection, while the corporation administered the town and Liberty, including its own property, and regulated trade. Constitutionally, following the Reformation of Henry VIII's reign, authority in spiritual matters (together with some lesser aspects of local administration) belonged to a Church of England of which the monarch was the titular head. The influence of the Anglican church in Berwick came to be dwarfed by that of the Presbyterians, however, with smaller communities of Methodists, Baptists and Catholics adding further diversity. Between them, the crown, corporation and church variously upheld, defended, imposed upon, constrained and regulated the lives and livelihoods of all Berwick's citizens, shaping their everyday experience and marking the urban landscape with symbols of authority and beneficence. The corporation and the various churches were also the main providers of education before the 20th century, when state provision made its first appearance in the town.

Church and crown, appropriately enough, have long combined forces in the north-east quarter of the walled town, where the Barracks faces Holy Trinity Church across the Parade (on which companies of soldiers were drilled) and the 18th-century vicarage looks on from the west. The Parade and churchyard, with their ample, regular spaces and air of ordered tranquillity, contrast with the close-packed bustle of the main commercial streets where the corporation's authority was centred in the Town Hall (Fig 32), located at the foot of Marygate on a site once occupied by a medieval market cross. During the 19th century, as Berwick's constitution was overhauled and in an atmosphere of growing religious tolerance, this visible separation of powers was blurred and a series of public and civic buildings took the place of some of the houses and alehouses formerly bordering the Parade. In 1848–9 the town gaol and court house (now the Municipal Buildings), an imposing mock-Elizabethan building, was built just next to the Parade in Wallace Green, providing a new home for some functions previously housed in the Town Hall in Marygate. A Church of England school was attached to the vicarage in 1856

Figure 32
Berwick's Town Hall was an emblem of the town's
power, prestige and independence.
[DP065206]

and in 1858–9 the Presbyterian church (since 1792 Church of Scotland) followed on the corner of Wallace Green and Parade. Built to designs by J D & I Hay of Liverpool, its assertive corner position and strident spire seem calculated to disparage and eclipse the low parish church behind it. Finally, a Masonic lodge was built on the corner of Church Street and Walkergate in 1871. By the end of the 19th century state, civic and ecclesiastical authority were all represented in equal measure and a more ecumenical spirit reigned.

Defence of the realm

The crown's role originated in the town's turbulent past and particularly in the need to secure it against the frequent resurgence of Scottish arms. The seat of power was the castle, which formed one extremity of the walled circuit built by Edward I but which also contained comfortable accommodation and stores as well as having the services of a nearby corn mill (*see* Fig 4). The origin of 'two lytel towers' on the Tweedmouth bank, noted in a survey of fortified sites made in 1541, is less clear, though the names of two houses – Tweedmouth Tower, Tower Road, and Tower House, Mount Road – appear to perpetuate their memory.[19]

Following the Reformation the risk of attack from Catholic powers on the Continent increased, but the medieval defences, designed before the advent of artillery, were vulnerable. Attempts to upgrade them under Henry VIII and Edward VI did no more than pick at the problem. Finally, at the start of Elizabeth's embattled reign, more systematic modernisation began. Adopting the bastion system of defence developed in Renaissance Italy, the new ramparts were designed to withstand an assault by the latest artillery and consisted of huge earthen banks revetted in stone on their outer face and defended at salient points by arrow-shaped bastions allowing the surrounding ditch to be raked by gunshot (*see* Fig 28). As ever in the crown's defence projects, funds were intermittent and in its final form the scheme retained the medieval walls where they ran along the riverside. The new defences were also much more tightly drawn around the core of the town, leaving the sparsely populated Greenses (about one-third of the area contained by the medieval walls) to fend for themselves in the event of attack. The medieval castle, now obsolete in its role as a citadel or refuge of last resort, was left outside the new defences, a mere quarry for building stone. In 1604 James I disposed of it to the corporation.[20]

On completion of the new ramparts, entry to the town was confined to four points: the English Gate or Bridge Gate facing the bridge and the London road; the Scotch Gate or Scots Gate on the road to Edinburgh; the Shore Gate, providing access to the town quay from the bottom of Sandgate; and the Cow Port, which led to the Magdalene Fields and, as its name suggests, was used to lead livestock to pasture (Fig 33). For security, these gates were narrow, allowing only a single cart to pass at a time; they were also closed at night to all traffic, wheeled and pedestrian, and manned by guards from the town's garrison. The Main Guard, a guardhouse which once stood inside the Scotch Gate but became redundant and was taken down and re-erected in Palace Street in 1815–16, survives to illustrate something of the nature of this system (*see* Fig 102).

The garrison, in accordance with normal 16th- and 17th-century practice, was quartered in the town's many alehouses. Whilst this brought welcome income to alehouse-keepers, the system was not without its problems: the crown was often in arrears with payments and if numbers rose (as they sometimes did in times of heightened anxiety) private citizens might be obliged to accommodate the surplus. Agitation against the practice from 1705 onwards led to the construction of the country's earliest surviving purpose-built barracks (1717–21), together with a suitably imposing Governor's House on Palace Green, where there had long been ordnance stores and magazines. The London architect Nicholas Hawksmoor (1661–1736) designed the Barracks, though there is no evidence that he was involved in the detailed execution of the work.

Hawksmoor's design brought a new order and scale to the Berwick scene (Fig 34). Two enormous barrack blocks, capable of holding nearly 700 men plus their commanding officers (though they were seldom more than half full in the 18th century), faced each other across a spacious yard in the centre of which stood a well house. The north end of the yard was closed by a screen wall and gateway while to the south a magazine and granaries were replaced, between 1739 and 1741, by a substantial new storehouse (now housing Berwick-upon-Tweed Museum & Art Gallery). Each barrack block was three storeys high and two rooms deep beneath an M-profile roof with prominent

Figure 33
The Cow Port is the only one of Berwick's Elizabethan gates to retain its original form.
[DP071113]

Figure 34
The Barracks from the air with the Cow Port in the foreground. The two long ranges and the low range containing the gate were completed in 1721; the storehouse to the rear replaced other buildings in 1739–41.
[NMR 20688/14]

crow-stepped gables. The crow-steps, significantly, do not appear on Hawksmoor's surviving drawings, which show a single roof span concealed by scrolled gable parapets; this suggests that those executing the work translated the costlier elements of his designs into familiar and less expensive Berwick idioms. Stone was taken from the now defunct castle to face the walls, which are predominantly of brick manufactured locally in Tweedmouth – by far the largest use of brick in the town by this date. The ordinary soldiers lived 8 men to a room in what were effectively a series of houses, each with 12 rooms and its own stair. The officers enjoyed more genteel accommodation in the bulkier blocks at the northern end of each barrack, presenting a formal front to the Parade where soldiers were drilled.

The Governor's House on the Ness in Palace Green seems oddly distant from the Barracks, but there was a long-established government depot in the

Figure 35
The Governor's House, as befitted the crown's representative, was the most substantial house within the town, with gardens stretching to the ramparts.

a) *(above, top) The Bucks' 1740s prospect shows it (numbered 19) before it was heightened to three storeys. [The South View of Berwick Upon Tweed, c 1743–45 by Samuel and Nathaniel Buck/Yale Center for British Art, Paul Mellon Collection/Bridgeman Art Library]*

b) *(above) The central portion of the Governor's House today.[DP071116]*

area (possibly, as Francis Cowe has suggested, reusing buildings of the former Carmelite friary). The Ness is flat and low-lying, the houses seeming to shelter beneath the ramparts. The Governor's House (Figs 35a and b) was perhaps the most imposing house in Berwick in its day, though a change in the colour of the masonry shows that its central block, currently three storeys high, was only two storeys originally (the Bucks' view confirms this analysis). Nevertheless it appeared tall, being raised over a basement to provide a *piano nobile* or raised principal storey; the flanking lower wings gave the street elevation an impressive horizontal extent, forming the whole of one side of the green. The latter dignifies the building's public face; to the rear there was a large garden extending eastwards as far as the ramparts and northwards to The Avenue. Architectural details tied the Governor's House to the Barracks. Solidity is conveyed by similarly bold, simple projecting piers and, before the present top storey was added (between 1746 and 1799), it had similar crow-stepped gables.

With the pacification of the Highlands after 1745 the last glimmers of a Scottish threat were extinguished and by the late 18th century Berwick's ramparts, though still operational, were again obsolete and increasingly given over to public recreation. The arms race triggered by the changing balance of European power – particularly the rise of a militaristic German state in the second half of the 19th century – posed new threats and large naval batteries

Figure 36 (left)
The Magdalene Fields army camp, established above
Greenses Haven north of Berwick in 1940, became
the nucleus of Berwick Holiday Park, the present
holiday camp.
[RAF 30050/PFFO-0016]

Figure 37 (right, top)
Holy Trinity Church was built to the designs of John
Young (d 1679), a London master mason, and was
completed in 1652. It is the most accomplished
17th-century building to survive in Berwick and is
notable for its early use of Serlian (also known as
Venetian) windows. The chancel projecting to the right
is a matching addition of 1855.
[DP065161]

Figure 38 (right)
Colonel George Fenwick of Brinkburn, Governor of
Berwick, was instrumental in ensuring that Holy Trinity
Church was built, bringing to an end half a century of
wrangling between the town and the state. His monument
is in the south aisle of the church.
[DP065612]

were installed to defend Berwick against hostile warships. And as invasion
threatened in 1940 a large army camp intended for 18 officers and 744 other
ranks was established on the clifftop above Greenses Haven (Fig 36); anti-
invasion defences also included concrete tank obstacles placed beneath the
arches of the Royal Border Bridge. Although Berwick's garrison ceased to exist
in 1964 part of the Barracks is still used by cadets and the lives and careers of
the soldiers stationed in the town are commemorated in the King's Own
Scottish Borderers Regimental Museum.

Competing faiths

The deserted medieval village of Bondington, which once overlooked the Tweed from Castle Terrace, is possibly Berwick's earliest Christian site north of the Tweed. St Mary's, Bondington, is thought to have been abandoned shortly after Edward I took the town in 1296. The dedication was duly transferred to a new church which in turn gave its name to Marygate, but this was demolished in the 1560s to make way for the Elizabethan ramparts. Holy Trinity Church (Fig 37) is also an early foundation, documented from *c* 1120; it stood next to the Parade just south of the present church. The latter is a rare example of a Cromwellian church and was built only after much lobbying, ultimately including the intervention of the town's governor, Colonel George Fenwick (Fig 38), about the inadequacy of the medieval church once St Mary's had been lost.

Church and state generally worked hand in hand in regulating behaviour and belief in 17th- and 18th-century England, as the proximity of the Barracks and parish church might seem to suggest, but in Berwick the reality was very different. The ministry in Berwick of the fiery Scottish Calvinist preacher John Knox between 1549 and 1551 is credited with disposing the townsfolk – freemen as well as common citizens – overwhelmingly towards Presbyterianism, which became the established church in Scotland but not in England. The town's first permanent Nonconformist place of worship – opened in 1719 and known for many years as the Low Meeting House – traced its descent from Knox's teachings; the later High Meeting House (1724) and Middle Meeting House (1756) catered for similar congregations (Fig 39). They brought the total number of seatings available to Presbyterians to some 3,000, roughly three times the number that could be accommodated at Holy Trinity Church. By this time Spittal already had its own meeting house (commemorated in Meeting House Yard), opened in 1752 on the site of the present St Paul's Church (1878). Tweedmouth acquired one at the far tip of

Figure 39
The Middle Meeting House, built in 1756, was the third of Berwick's four 18th-century Presbyterian chapels and is the oldest to survive. It was recently threatened with demolition. However, an investigation into the history of the building identified its significance despite extensive alterations. The building now has planning permission to convert it to offices.
[DP065725]

West End in 1783. Subsequent growth was fuelled by factionalism. For instance, later in the 18th century the Middle Meeting House, while remaining doctrinally the same, took issue on a point of church government (specifically the right to appoint its own ministers) and became known as the Relief Meeting House. The Burgher Meeting House was built in Golden Square in 1770 and proved so popular that it had to be enlarged in 1796. The Anti-Burghers, who refused to countenance the Burgher Oath whereby holders of public office endorsed the established church, met in a school in Marygate before 1812, when they acquired their own chapel behind Church Street. Further secessions followed (Fig 40) and this trend was only reversed in the late 19th century as depleted congregations amalgamated.

The early meeting houses were plain, capacious boxes – and they were difficult to fit into an urban landscape that was already densely built up. Characteristically they found a foothold in the yards to the rear of houses and inns. The Low Meeting House occupied the yard behind the Brown Bear public house, the High Meeting House was situated in Red Lion Yard off Marygate and the Middle Meeting House fronted Chapel Street, a far from prestigious back way (then called Shaw's Lane) running behind Marygate. Berwick's first post-Reformation Catholic church, Our Blessed Lady and St Cuthbert, followed a similar course, opening in a yard off Church Street and moving to another off Ravensdowne in 1829.

Prior to 1829 the authority of the Church of England was bolstered by the fact that non-communicants were disqualified from public office (though many, including some freemen, resorted to token attendances). By the mid-19th century the established church had to compete like any other for souls. Holy Trinity Church was re-ordered in 1855 and the dedication to St Mary's was revived for a new church in Castlegate, built 1857–8 to serve the swelling population of the northern part of the town. In 1871 Spittal was provided with its own church, St John the Evangelist on Main Street (Fig 41), and was declared a parish in its own right for the first time. All these churches received benefactions in the form of furnishings and glass from parishioners and others associated with the town. Among these pride of place must be given to Holy Trinity's reredos – in 1893 Miss Ramsey L'Amy commissioned the young Edwin Lutyens (1869–1944) to design this ornamental screen in memory of her parents (Fig 42).

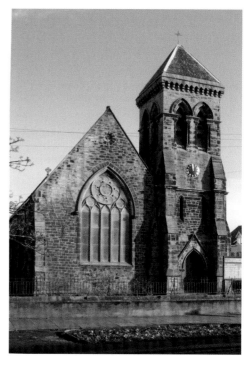

Figure 41 (above)
St John the Evangelist signalled Spittal's rise to parish status. Thought to be the work of John Howison, a Newcastle architect, it was consecrated in 1871 and the tower was added in 1894.
[DP071123]

Berwick corporation and local government

The town's administrative affairs were vested in the corporation, which was also responsible for policing and, to an extent unusual among English towns, the administration of justice (Fig 43). The corporation's building activity in the town stemmed from three main sources. First, there was the need (under its royal charter) to supplement income from its own property with a variety of tolls (especially from markets and wharfage, both of which it regulated

Figure 42 (right)
The reredos in Holy Trinity Church dates from 1893 and is one of Edwin Lutyens' earliest works. In 1902 he returned to the area to work at nearby Lindisfarne Castle.
[DP065616]

jealously) and this entailed maintaining a harbour and other infrastructure. Second, until 1835 the corporation was obliged to meet the particular needs of its constituents – the freemen – most notably in education, and to ensure the general well-being of all the town's citizens, provided this did not result in unacceptable financial burdens for the freemen. Third, these straightforward motives were increasingly coloured by a desire to promote the town's dignity, especially in the widening world of trade.

The corporation's great monument is the Town Hall (*see* Fig 32), built in two phases between 1750 and 1761 to replace an earlier building on the same site. It combined the functions of a guildhall, an election chamber for the mayor and (until 1832) the town's two MPs, a court room, assembly room (Fig 44), gaol, debtor's prison (Figs 45 and 46) and covered market. Once again London expertise, in the shape of designs by Samuel and John Worrall, was called in, but a Berwick carpenter, Joseph Dods, superintended the work (though in an inscription he is proclaimed the architect). The Town Hall stands

Figure 43 (below, left)
Justice presides over the former courtroom in the Town Hall. The plaster relief dates from 1770.
[DP065672]

Figure 44 (below, right)
The Town Hall's capacious assembly room remains one of the town's premier venues for social events.
[DP065669]

Figure 45 (above)
In the Town Hall's austere attic storey debtors and
felons were confined under regimes of varying severity.
This view shows one of the two condemned cells.
[DP065683]

Figure 46 (right)
Debtors, as readers of Charles Dickens's Little Dorrit
will recall, enjoyed liberties denied to felons. In Berwick
they were entitled to take the air on the rooftop of the
Town Hall.
[DP071092]

Figure 47
Mayoral or corporation inscriptions occur frequently in Berwick, but not in Tweedmouth or Spittal, where their authority did not extend until 1835. This example proclaims the Corporation Academy of 1798 (now the Leaping Salmon public house).
[DP071121]

in the heart of the ancient marketplace, confirming the corporation's allegiance to the town's trade, but it has something of the appearance of a City of London church with its porticoed front and tall steeple adorned with superimposed classical orders. Indeed the steeple (also a feature of many Scottish tollbooths) made good a deficiency of the parish church, incorporating a clock and a peal of bells that were tolled to summon the church congregation.

The corporation was the principal provider of education in Berwick from the 17th century, when the Grammar School was founded, to the 19th century, remaining active in the field until the inter-war years when its schools were finally absorbed into the state system. While the Grammar School provided a classical grounding, much of the corporation's educational effort went into providing basic literacy and numeracy skills: at the end of the 18th century separate writing, reading and mathematical schools were amalgamated to form the Corporation Academy on Bank Hill (Fig 47). The children of freemen were entitled to free schooling at such establishments; for the poor the Charity

Figure 48
The Charity or Blue Coat School on Ravensdowne, as rebuilt in 1842.
[DP065218]

or Blue Coat School (after the uniform of the scholars) was established in 1725 by one Captain Bolton on Ravensdowne, where it was rebuilt in its present form in 1842 (Fig 48). From the early 19th century educational provision proliferated; schools maintained by church congregations became more common, the National and British School movements opened establishments and there were also a series of small, often short-lived, schools based in private houses.

4

Commercial growth: Berwick looks abroad

Berwick's natural hinterland straddles the Anglo-Scottish border. It is, and always has been, a thinly populated and largely agricultural area, with just a sprinkling of small market towns – Belford and Wooler on the English side, Coldstream, Duns, Kelso and Eyemouth in Scotland – catering for essentially local needs. There was little local competition for the resulting coastal trade. The nearest harbours – at Burnmouth and Eyemouth to the north and Budle Bay, Holy Island and Beadnell to the south – were minnows compared to Berwick, but its main regional competitors, Newcastle and Leith, were another matter.

The best of the agricultural land (judging by the distribution of the towns) follows the Tweed, the upper course of which lies wholly in Scotland. The history of Berwick's fluctuating trade is closely linked to the progress of Anglo-Scottish relations. Under Scottish rule the medieval town enjoyed considerable prosperity, attributable in large part to the export of wool – on a scale substantial enough to attract Venetian merchants. Once it became an English possession, however, its hinterland was halved since the imposition of excise duties placed much of the best agricultural land effectively beyond reach. These duties remained in force long after the union of the English and Scottish crowns, disappearing only with the parliamentary Act of Union of 1707. Thereafter Berwick experienced a surge of prosperity lasting a generation and this had a profound impact on the appearance of the town, especially in Bridge Street, Sandgate, Hide Hill and Marygate, where merchants and their premises were concentrated. The place of wool as the mainstay of Berwick's commerce had by now been taken by the lucrative salmon trade (Fig 49), but there were other opportunities for enterprising freemen, notably in the herring fishery and in the growing exports of cereals and other agricultural produce.

The fisheries for salmon, herring and other fish were the most prized natural resources of Berwick, Tweedmouth and Spittal. Well into the 19th century fish represented Berwick's most valuable commodity (Fig 50). The sea provided a seemingly inexhaustible harvest of herring and the Tweed and its seaward approaches yielded the far more valuable salmon as it returned from its adult life at sea to its spawning grounds upriver. Fish could be dried, salted, smoked, pickled or packed in ice for preservation; shipped in barrels or boxes (known as 'kits') it formed an important part of the diet of towns all along the coast and often well inland. London's appetite for Tweed salmon was

Figure 49
Salmon being landed on the Tweedmouth shore: a detail from View of the Town and Bridge of Berwick*, which was engraved by F Jukes after an original by C Catton Jnr and published in 1793.* [British Library Board, All Rights Reserved, Maps K.Top.32.47.e]

insatiable, especially once the availability of ice allowed fresh fish to be traded. Over the centuries the buildings and other structures required to catch, preserve and pack fish have left a decisive mark on the town and its neighbouring settlements, and along the banks of the Tweed.

The salmon fishery

The special importance of the salmon is reflected in the control of fishing rights stretching from the Tweed's seaward approaches upstream to Norham and beyond (Fig 51). The fishery operated seasonally from January to October. Since the approach of the salmon could occur at any time of the day and night, and since many stretches of the river were remote from permanent settlements, fishing 'shiels' were built along the river bank, providing a lodging for the fishermen and a place to store their nets and other equipment. The name 'shiel' has its origin (together with variants such as 'shieling' and 'scale') in Norse farming practices a millennium ago, usually referring to the seasonal dwellings of pastoral farmers who took their herds to higher pastures during the summer months so that the lower lying land could be cropped for hay.

The majority of the shiels known from 19th-century maps can still be identified today. A few have been converted to permanent dwellings or holiday homes, but most are now disused and many are ruinous. The earliest surviving examples may date from the first half of the 18th century or even earlier. They are small single-storey buildings, with a single room entered by a doorway against one gable and heated by a hearth on the other. The hearth provided warmth, allowed hot food and drinks to be prepared and helped to dry nets and other gear that would perish if left constantly damp. In some of the earliest examples the hearth is expressed externally as a shallow apsidal projection. Typically the interior is lit by a single small window placed in the same wall as the entrance, facing the river.

The smallness of the window is a clue to the fact that the fishermen did not keep watch from the shiel. By the 19th century if not before, this was done from a watch-box (or 'fording box'), which might take one of a number of forms. Some resembled the crow's nest of a ship, attached to the gable of the

Figure 50 (above)
The importance of the salmon fishery to Berwick's prosperity is underlined by the details depicted on a banknote issued by the Tweed Bank based at 22 and 24 Hide Hill. The salmon lookout known as Bailey Batt is prominent on the left, fishermen draw in a net on the right and a Berwick smack, doubtless laden with salmon, heads for the open sea.
[By permission of Berwick-upon-Tweed Corporation (Freemen) Trustees, DP065680]

Figure 51 (right)
The 1837 Plan of Berwick Harbour and sea coast to the south; with Plan of the Fishing Nets &c, from which this detail is taken, gives considerable information on the salmon fisheries in the Tweed estuary and its seaward approaches, including the positions of shiels (labelled 'shields' on this plan) and ice houses and an indication of the kinds of nets used.
[Berwick-upon-Tweed Museum & Art Gallery, DP065595]

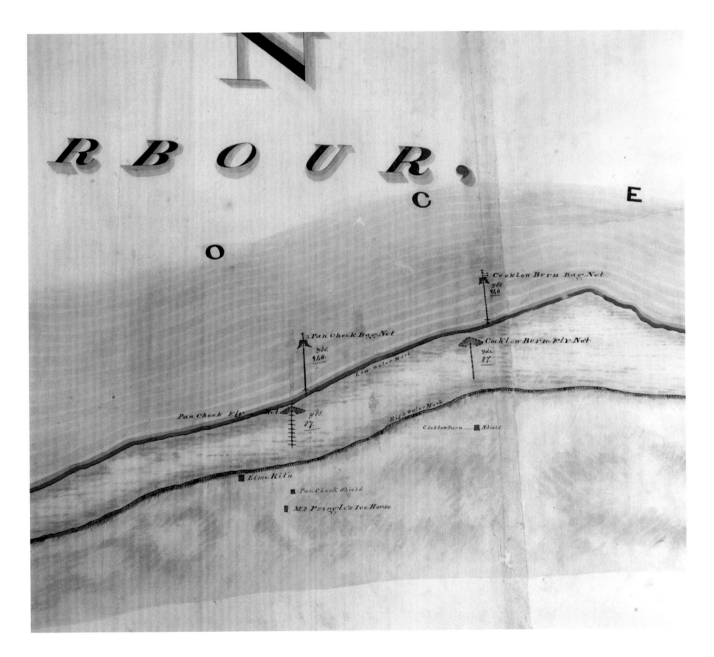

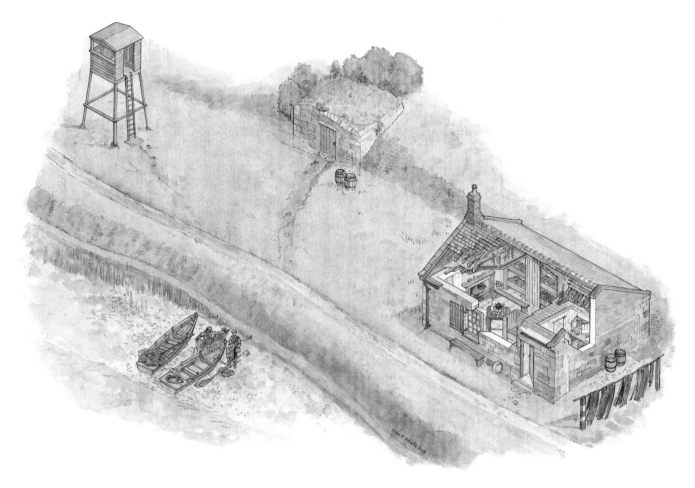

shiel. Others took the form of a free-standing timber tower on which a viewing
platform was mounted (Fig 52). Free-standing watch-boxes were invariably
placed downstream of the shiel so as to give advance warning of the salmon's
approach; on the lookout's shouted signal the fishermen would emerge
from the shiel, rush to their coble (a flat-bottomed, high-bowed, clinker-built
boat) and row into the stream to set their nets in the path of the oncoming
salmon. The catch (minus an allowance for the men's own needs) would be
kept cool and by the 19th century this was being done with the aid of a small
purpose-built store resembling a miniature ice house, usually built into
sloping ground close to the river bank.

Figure 52
*This reconstruction, based on Low Bells Shiel,
shows a larger-scale shiel accompanied by a
vaulted store and watch-box.*

In 1859, at the former Ethermouth Shiel near the confluence of the Whiteadder and the Tweed, the travel writer Walter White found seven or eight men sharing a one-roomed shiel with the use of two boats. The fishermen, hired by the owner or operator of the fishery, worked as a gang for wages in money and in kind (salmon), spending a continuous six-day stretch at the shiel (fishing being forbidden on Sundays). In the remoter shiels the men might be supplied with food and other items by small boat; the same boats would deliver ice and carry the catch downriver to Berwick.[21]

Shiels are not unvarying in character. In Spittal there is a pair of shiels, both on a larger scale than normal, but both having just one hearth and one small window (Fig 53). They now have a slate roof, but the tall upstanding gables are clearly intended for a thatched roof and it is likely that all early shiels were similarly thatched. Generous proportions are more characteristic of later shiels, where typically an entrance lobby and separate net store are partitioned off from the principal room. These larger shiels seem to date from the middle of the 19th century and later, and they often have two windows in

Figure 53
These paired fishing shiels (probably early 18th century) on Sandstell Road, Spittal, are among the earliest surviving. The form of the roof shows that they were once thatched.
[DP065264]

the front wall. At Under Greenhill, towards Norham, a red-brick shiel with concrete lintels, steel-framed windows and a shallow-pitched felt roof is a surprising sight; its arrangements do not differ in essentials from those of the larger 19th-century shiels and it demonstrates the persistence of traditional practices well into the 20th century.

The salmon trade was profitable primarily because it satisfied a demand outside the locality, principally in London (Fig 54). In 1756 a writer noted the export of eggs and butter from Berwick, but reserved the greater part of his commentary for the trade in Tweed salmon, which was reckoned

> the best in the kingdom; great quantities of this fish, being pickled, is put up in vessels called kits by persons who subsist wholly by that employment and are called salmon coopers, and then shipped off to London; considerable quantities of the smaller fish are also sent to London alive, in vessels called smacks, which are built for that purpose, having a well in the middle bored full of holes for the free passage of the sea water, in which the fish are conveyed without injury; these vessels are also reckoned very safe for passengers, as they will lie nearer the wind, and bear heavier seas than any other. At Berwick the best salmon may be bought for a penny a pound during the months of June and July, but at some other parts of the year it bears a considerable price.[22]

Berwick's salmon trade was in the hands of the town's master coopers whose trade, nominally at least, was the making of the barrels and kits in which fish were packed. According to Fuller, there were 32 salmon coopers in Berwick in 1799.[23] The 27 master coopers mentioned in Good's 1806 *Directory* are therefore likely to be something like a complete list. Good lists 12 with premises in Bridge Street, 8 in West Street, 4 in Sandgate and 3 on the Quay Walls.[24] Such a remarkable concentration reflected the corporation's strict regulation of trade, which meant that shipments could only be made from the quayside.

For most of the 18th century the salmon was transported pickled or boiled. But in 1788 the continental practice of shipping fresh fish in ice was adopted and, in order to maintain stocks of ice through the salmon season, a number of ice houses were built in the town. The one on Bank Hill dates from *c* 1796 and

Figure 54
Salmon was transported to London in smacks such as this one. The painting, which is on 18th-century panelling, was formerly in the King's Arms Hotel and is now displayed in the Town Hall.
[By permission of Berwick-upon-Tweed Corporation (Freemen) Trustees, DP065678]

Figure 55
The enormous ice house on Bank Hill, built around 1796, is now cared for by the Berwick Preservation Trust. After ice ceased to be used commercially in the salmon trade, the ice house was linked by new doorways and stairs to properties standing above it.
[DP065713]

is typical enough, being built into a hillside (the covering of earth acting as an insulating layer) and having a high vaulted ceiling and a flat floor (Fig 55). This last characteristic differentiates them from most country house ice houses, which had spherical or egg-shaped chambers. Ice was initially gathered from local watercourses and ponds, but increasingly the demand was met by imports from Norway. Other ice houses survive on the east side of Ravensdowne, where the disturbed ground to the rear of the ramparts was piled over the masonry vaults (Fig 56).

Declining salmon stocks led to the demise of the salmon fishery in the late 20th century. Its last days were evocatively captured by local photographer Jim Walker, but the remaining buildings face an uncertain future (Fig 57).

Figure 56 (above)
Disturbed or made-up ground between the ramparts and Ravensdowne was relatively easy to excavate or heap up around a masonry vault. Here an ice house entrance pops up incongruously among allotments.
[DP065165]

Figure 57 (right)
The former premises of the Berwick Salmon Fisheries Company in Sandstell Road, Spittal.
[DP065654]

The herring fishery

The humble herring could never be the making of Berwick's fortune in the same way as the salmon. Its teeming shoals have been pursued by fishermen all along Britain's coast for centuries but fresh, pickled or smoked (as kippers) it has never commanded premium prices. Its cheapness, on the other hand, made it a staple food for the poor, and the scale of operation needed to feed this demand was large.

Once the fish was ashore only a small proportion was sold fresh to local buyers in Berwick's daily fish market and elsewhere. The remainder would be pickled or smoked and shipped to markets elsewhere. Pickling was monopolised by the powerful coopers of Berwick, but curing was already being undertaken on a large scale in Tweedmouth before the end of the 18th century. During the 19th century Spittal became the main centre of production. The largest establishment was Robert Boston's (known as Boston Brothers by the early 20th century) on Sandstell Road, which employed up to 100 workers at its peak and possessed long ranges of curing sheds (Fig 58). Small smokehouses were also put up in yards behind some of the houses in Berwick, Tweedmouth and Spittal (Fig 59). These were tall buildings with a rooftop louvre and filled with a light wooden framework from which fish could be suspended. The sharp decline of the herring fishery in the 1930s was attributed to overfishing.

The Greenland whale fishery

Strictly 'whale fishery' is a misnomer, since whales are mammals, but the phrase was widely used to describe the dangerous, but potentially lucrative, hunting of whales off the coast of Greenland in the late 18th and 19th centuries. Whales, especially the aptly named right whale, were sought principally for the oil which could be derived from their blubber. In an age that had yet to discover mineral oil, whale oil was highly esteemed as a lubricant and for lighting.

Berwick's role in the whaling trade was small compared with major players such as Hull, Leith and even Whitby, but it preserves two significant reminders from this era (Figs 60 and 61). On John Wood's 1823 map of Berwick, an 'Oil

Figure 58
Gable end of a single-storey open-fronted curing shed. This was one of two concrete and corrugated-iron ranges built for the Tweed Fishery Works of Boston Brothers by Spittal builders A C Burns to designs dated March 1908. [DP071138]

Figure 59
Few of the once numerous smokehouses in Berwick, Tweedmouth and Spittal survive in recognisable form. One of the last to have been used is this example in Bridge Street, identifiable externally by its louvre. [DP071137]

Figure 60 (above)
The former oil house of the Berwick Whale Fishing Co,
later extended to serve as a maltings. The oil house
formed the eight bays to the right of the cart entrance
in the three-storey range facing the sea.
[DP065611]

Figure 61 (right)
John M Dickson, manager of the Berwick Whale Fishing
Co, lived at 1 Wellington Row (see Fig 68), where the
front door panels incorporate a harpoon motif.
[DP065208]

House' is clearly marked alongside Pier Road. The building's exposed position beyond the town ramparts was well suited to the smelly process of rendering down whale blubber. The Pier Road oil house was adapted and extended to serve as a maltings before 1837, which may explain the existence of a similarly isolated oil house, now demolished, by that date on what is now North Greenwich Road, Spittal. Berwick's short-lived whaling trade came to an end in 1838 when the stores of the *Norfolk* were auctioned at the Spittal oil yard following two successive unproductive seasons.[25]

The grain trade

Vying for space with the coopers in the Bridge Street area of Berwick were the corn merchants, whose multi-storey grain warehouses or granaries were a distinctive feature. The best-known survivor of this much depleted building type is the five-storey, mid-18th-century Dewar's Lane granary (*see* Fig 21) formerly belonging to the firm of Dewar & Carmichael, though there is another example in West Street. Granaries converted to residential use can be found in Love Lane and on Quay Walls, while another granary was remodelled to form the Maltings Arts Centre, which opened in 1990. They were simple, robust buildings, usually with floors supported on huge axial beams and storey posts of Baltic pine, ventilated by small openings fitted with wooden shutters. Ideally they enjoyed direct communication with the quayside: the Dewar's Lane example is notable for the survival of a small tramway passing through an opening in the defensive wall.

Corn merchants benefited from improvements in agricultural practices, in which north Northumberland was something of a leader. In the 1790s it was noted that the 'spirit of improvement in agriculture has extended itself greatly over this quarter'; 'barren wastes' had been enclosed, new farmsteads built and 'the lands so well cultivated' – particularly by the introduction of turnip rotations – 'as to produce very good corn and grass'.[26] Tweedmouth and Spittal Moors, hitherto common land covered in heath, were among the areas enclosed at about this time,[27] and the early presence of two threshing engines in Tweedmouth is further evidence of innovative practices.[28] These threshing engines were probably horse-powered, but during the 19th century

Figure 62
The area of Berwick between Quay Walls and Marygate was photographed on 30 April 1949, when the large multi-storey granaries still dominated their surroundings.
[AFL03/Aerofilms/A22832]

the surrounding area was notable for the use of steam power for a range of agricultural uses.

By the early 19th century the grain trade had transformed the appearance of the town between the Quay Walls and Bridge Street and onwards, up the steep slope of the brae, into the area bounded by Hide Hill and Marygate (Fig 62). Typically rising four or five storeys, darkening the narrow streets in which they were located and threaded by alleys and tunnels, the granaries added drama to a streetscape already rendered striking by the long, narrow plots contained within the high ramparts.

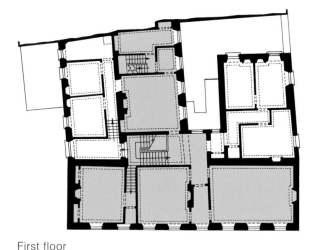

First floor

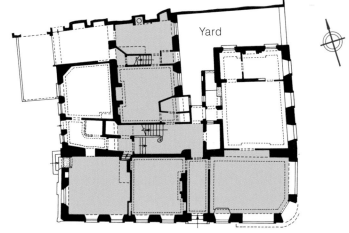

Yard

Ground floor

2 0   10 m

10 0   30 ft

The rebuilding of Berwick

The rebuilding of Berwick seems to have gathered pace at about the time that the Barracks and the Governor's House were being built. These imposing new buildings are likely to have inspired Berwick's wealthier residents with a vision of a new form of architecture – taller, more substantial and more regular than the prevailing styles – and building continued throughout the 18th and early 19th centuries, despite periodic slack trade owing to wars and competition from other ports (Figs 63a and b). Better and more frequent links with the outside world made the town more receptive to innovation. The new houses had slated or pantiled roofs and regular sashed elevations, though the symmetry of many was disrupted by an off-centre entrance or a yard entrance at one end, in some cases perpetuating earlier arrangements. Their owners built to enjoy the comforts that their wealth opened up to them, to show their acquaintance with the latest architectural fashions and to demonstrate the solidity of their businesses, the premises of which often stood just to the rear (Figs 64a and b).

Figure 63 2 Love Lane, Berwick.

a) (left, top) This house was built c 1760, probably by a prosperous merchant. The accommodation, later extended, originally comprised a two-storey street range and a three-storey rear range;

b) (left) the principal stair is built on a generous scale. [DP065331]

Figure 64 Some of Berwick's 18th-century houses retain fine interior fittings.

a) (above, left) At 57 West Street this mid-18th-century chimneypiece and overmantel adorn a first-floor drawing room; the chimney board – a rare survival – is designed to cover the opening during the summer months. [DP065380]

b) (above, right) 5 Ness Street, a smaller house of c 1770, has a simple and compact 'Chinese Chippendale' stair. [DP065586]

In the course of the 18th century Berwick grew to be a major port for coastwise shipping and began to acquire a more significant stake in overseas trade. Towards the end of the century, however, the town's importance as a border garrison diminished sharply and although it remained part of the chain of coastal defences – in a state of heightened anxiety from the 1790s until 1815 – military control weakened. The area near the Quay was a particular beneficiary of the change. Along the southern end of the Bridge Street plots, where granaries and other commercial premises were tightly hemmed in by the quayside rampart, many seized the opportunity to built atop the rampart, transforming Berwick from a town sheltering within its defensive walls to one looking confidently outwards (Fig 65).

Many of Berwick's wealthier citizens were members of the professions, office-holders of one sort or another or individuals (including many women) living on investments or annuities. Such people, as well as those military

officers who did not choose to reside in the quarters provided for them at the Barracks, had no need to live in the commercial heart of the town, which became cramped with the development of court housing on the back lots and was filled with everyday noises and smells. They were able to exploit instead the quieter backwaters where more space could be had for gardens (Fig 66) and where fresh air and extensive views might be enjoyed. In this they were assisted by the progressive demilitarisation of the ramparts, which rendered particularly attractive those properties lying on the eastern side of Ravensdowne and Palace Street East, the latter already dignified at its southern end by the presence of the Governor's House with its extensive garden. Ravensdowne, which in the 17th century was stigmatised as Ratten

Figure 65
Mostly late 18th and early 19th century houses rise above the Elizabethan ramparts to enjoy an unobstructed prospect across the River Tweed to Tweedmouth and Spittal. The ramparts survive as an elevated pedestrian street.
[DP065177]

Figure 66
Behind 7 Ravensdowne lies an unexpectedly large
garden. Here, probably in the early 19th century, a
south-facing brick garden wall was built, incorporating
an arched recess for a timber summerhouse, now lost.
[DP065588]

Figure 67
These houses at the lower end of Ravensdowne, built in the early decades of the 19th century at a time when the status of the street was rising rapidly, are among the most opulent in the town.
[DP065190]

Row (from the Scottish and northern dialect word 'ratten' or 'ratton', a rat) and in the 18th century was referred to dismissively as Back Way, became the premier residential address for professional people and others in the early decades of the 19th century under the short-lived name of Union Street (Fig 67). Wellington Row, overlooking the estuary, was a similar beneficiary of this early 19th-century 'peace dividend' (Fig 68).

By the early 19th century the preferred residence for better-off business or professional people was the villa – a detached or semi-detached house located on the outskirts of town with ample gardens to front and rear, and preferably an attractive landscape prospect. The local standard was set by Castle Hills House (Fig 69), built around 1830 for the Askews of Pallinsburn. The house occupied the former Spring Gardens, sloping steeply down to the Tweed,

Figure 68
Wellington Row stands above the rampart facing straight across the Tweed, heedless of potential foreign aggressors – Wellington had put them to flight. Though the three houses are outwardly similar, two (left and centre) were described as newly built in 1816 and No 1 (left) was occupied by John M Dickson, manager of the Berwick Whale Fishing Co. The third, which served as the manse for the former Presbyterian Secession Church (formerly the Burgher Meeting House) in Golden Square and then for Wallace Green Presbyterian Church, was not built until after 1844. [DP065209]

which was celebrated in the late 18th century for its extensive views of Berwick, the Tweed and Holy Island (Fig 70). Shortly afterwards villas began to be built on Castle Terrace, which extended along the brink of the same steep slope towards Castle Hills House and Duns. Ava Lodge was the first and most substantial of these villas, built shortly before 1840 and home in 1855 to a naval captain, William Smith. Nearest the town some of the sloping ground was common land, crossed by fishermen using the fishing boat depot under Carlin Brae, and this circumstance helped to preserve the spacious setting of the villas that proliferated during the middle and later years of the 19th century (*see* Fig 11).

5 The rise of industry

Industry and housing: the 19th and 20th centuries

The progress of industrial development in Berwick-upon-Tweed followed a familiar pattern. Like most small provincial towns it acquired a range of industries satisfying local and regional needs (Fig 71). Many of these industries processed agricultural products or by-products: corn-milling, malting and brewing, tanning and shoemaking. Other concerns, such as sawmills and foundries, were dependent upon imported raw materials. Some, like cabinet-making or watch-making, serviced a wealthy elite. And Berwick, like most seaports, developed maritime industries such as boat- and ship-building, rope-making and sailcloth manufacture. During the 18th century few of these enterprises were conducted on a large scale, but towards 1800, echoing developments elsewhere in the country, there was a noticeable change. James Good, writing in 1806, remarked upon 'the many and great improvements, that have taken place in Berwick within these last Twenty Years' as well as the rapid progress of industrial development in Tweedmouth 'within these last fifteen years', including the first steam corn mill in the area and Messrs Sibbit & Co's large brewery in Tweedmouth.[29]

Many activities, such as spinning, weaving and shoe-making were conducted largely in the home on the out-working principle. Slightly more elaborate undertakings were often sited in the yards behind street frontage houses: here subsequent clearances have been extensive. Messrs Sibbit & Co's Tweedmouth brewery is the most substantial survival of this era (Fig 72). But there were other large industrial buildings and complexes which have not survived. In 1793 Thomas Cockburn, who already ran a water-powered snuff mill at New Water Haugh, opened a sacking manufactory close to Bell Tower. Pleasantly situated, making 'a very handsome appearance' with 'a beautiful area in front', it was four storeys high, measured 100 by 20 feet and employed 80–100 men, women and children operating hand-powered looms using hemp imported from Baltic seaports.[30] Some large-scale concerns operated within Berwick's walls – there was another large brewery in Silver Street by the 1790s and there were numerous substantial grain warehouses – but increasingly Tweedmouth, Spittal and the Greenses were favoured for more substantial industrial developments because space was easier to find and there were fewer powerful voices to object to any resulting noise, smells or other pollution.

Figure 71
An Aerofilms view, taken on 3 October 1932, shows the dense concentration of industrial enterprises – mostly manure factories – on Spittal Point.
[AFL03/Aerofilms/40670]

Figure 72 (left)
Messrs Sibbit & Co's Tweedmouth brewery was established by the 1790s and survived (as the Border Brewery) until recent years. It is now a joinery works.
[DP065281]

Figure 73 (right)
The Sea View Iron Works, Main Street, Spittal (now Martin's Printing Works) the only foundry to survive, it was originally established to manufacture spades and shovels.
[DP065633]

Figure 74 (below)
A dated column base from Robert Ramsey's Tweedmouth ironworks, part of the porch of Tower House (formerly Tower Villa), Tweedmouth.
[DP065637]

Another industry that was to attain a degree of prominence in Berwick was iron manufacture. Smithies working imported iron would have been essential to the town's economy from an early date (by the 18th century iron was being imported from Scandinavia), but no foundries existed until about 1800 when John Robertson & Co established the Tower Foundry close to one of the former defensive towers on the east side of Tweedmouth.[31] By the 1820s the firm had prospered enough to have established (in partnership with one Robert Guthrie) a second foundry close to West End; about 1838 Guthrie opened another in Main Street, Spittal, on the large plot now occupied by the primary school. In 1855 Thomas Black, whose family had operated Ford Forge at Heatherslaw since 1769, built the Sea View Iron Works further along Main Street (Fig 73). Black's is the only ironworks to survive, but decorative and structural ironwork from other producers survives in a number of buildings (Fig 74).

The industrial development of Tweedmouth and Spittal is inextricably bound up with improvements in communications. The shallow bed and changeable regime of the Tweed made it unsuitable for inland navigation by boats larger than the salmon fishermen's flat-bottomed cobles and an early waggonway scheme, authorised in 1811 to link Spittal and Tweedmouth with

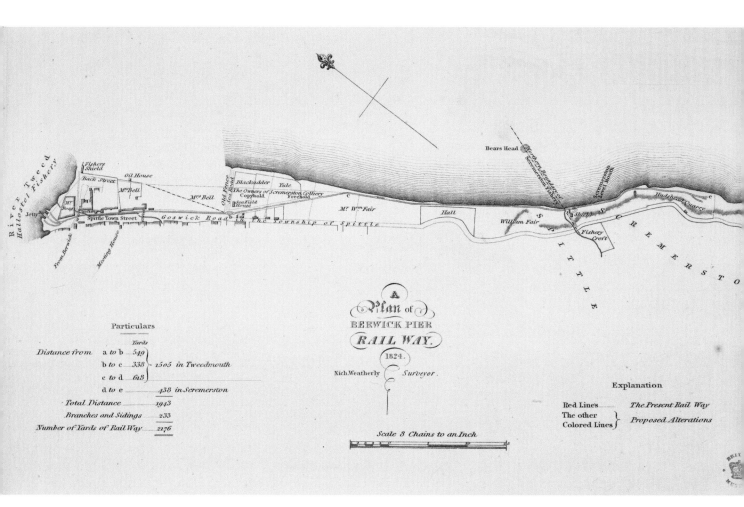

Figure 75
Plan of Berwick Pier Railway, *prepared for the Greenwich Hospital Estate in 1824, shows a proposed diversion (never actually executed) of this horse-drawn mineral waggonway. The actual route extends (from right to left) along the coast, turning inland along what is now South Greenwich Road, then along 'Goswick Road' and 'Spittle Town Street' (both now part of Main Street) on its way to the jetty.*
[British Library Board, All Rights Reserved, Maps 18.c.13.(132)]

The impact of the railway's arrival was felt widely in Berwick and Tweedmouth. The name Railway Street was bestowed after 1861 on an existing road connecting Berwick's station with the town centre.
[DP065727]

Kelso, remained unrealised.[32] About the same time, however, the Berwick Pier Railway, a horse-drawn waggonway, was built to carry stone from the Huds Head Quarry in the cliffs south of Spittal for the construction of the new Berwick Pier (commenced *c* 1810); the track was later extended via a gravity-operated incline to serve a number of collieries in Scremerston. From Huds Head Quarry it ran along the coast at the foot of the cliffs until it reached Far Sea Shiel on the outskirts of Spittal; here it turned inland until it joined Main Street, along the seaward side of which it proceeded as far as a staithe on the river (Fig 75; *see also* Fig 94).

The arrival of steam-hauled locomotion in the mid-1840s spelled the end for the Berwick Pier Railway but it gave an added impetus to industrial development. Although Berwick named a street in the railway's honour (Fig 76), it was Tweedmouth and Spittal that benefited most from its presence. In 1847 Tweedmouth Station (little more than the gate piers survive) opened just off what is now Northumberland Road and rapidly attracted a considerable concentration of industrial activity (Fig 77). Foremost among these enterprises were the Tweed Sawmills of Allan Brothers, timber and slate

Figure 77
Tweedmouth's Jacobethan station was demolished in the late 1960s as freight deserted the railways and Tweedmouth ceased to be a railway junction.
[OP001469]

Figure 78
Allan Brothers' Tweed Sawmills on Northumberland Road, Tweedmouth, was among the largest industrial enterprises in the Berwick area. Shortly after the railway's arrival it adopted a site close to Tweedmouth Station, a short siding (visible centre left) allowing timber to be brought in and out of the site by rail. It is captured here in an Aerofilms shot of 3 October 1932. [AFL03/Aerofilms/40657]

Figure 79
The manager's house of the Berwick & Tweedmouth Gaslight Co Ltd. (See Fig 71 for a sense of the wider complex before it was swept away.) [DP065650]

merchants, who transferred their business from Eyemouth to Tweedmouth between 1852 and 1855 (Fig 78). Steam-powered, and served by a railway siding, the huge Tweed Sawmills epitomised industry in the railway age. Only lengths of the high stone perimeter wall survive, enclosing what is now a large retail park.

After many years of anxious debate about the need for a wet dock large enough to accommodate the new steamships, Tweed Dock opened to vessels of up to 500 tons in 1876, decisively tilting the balance of benefits towards industries located on the Tweedmouth side of the river. The North Eastern Railway (successor to the originating companies) promptly built a switchback spur by which locomotives could descend from Tweedmouth to the dock. Tweedmouth was now more than ever the working heart of Berwick, a situation perhaps epitomised by the emergence at the end of the century of the Tweedside Co-operative Society Ltd, whose once extensive premises are now turned to other uses.

Spittal, though it now lacked a railway connection of its own, was also the scene of a remarkable industrial expansion (see Fig 71). At the beginning of the 19th century Spittal Point was almost bare but from the 1840s it rapidly filled up. One of the earliest arrivals was the Berwick & Tweedmouth Gaslight Co Ltd on North Greenwich Road (its competitor, the Berwick-upon-Tweed Gas Light Co, was founded in 1821 and was located in what became Oil Mill Lane, Berwick). The Berwick & Tweedmouth Gaslight Co Ltd works, opened in 1844, have been swept away but the contemporary manager's house survives (Fig 79). In the succeeding half century the area became dominated by no less than four chemical manure works, not to mention the North of England Works, which manufactured vitriol. For such enterprises, Spittal Point was ideal, as most of the time the prevailing south-westerly winds carried the smell out to sea.

Housing the poor

Industrial expansion at first did little to improve the living conditions of ordinary people. There was indeed a long history of poor housing in Berwick and Northumberland generally – poor at least by comparison with the standards deemed normal further south. In the 1720s Daniel Defoe was struck by the way in which conditions in Northumberland were more reminiscent of Scotland than of England:

> … even the buildings in the towns, and in the villages imitate the Scots almost all over Northumberland; witness their building the houses with the stairs (to the second floor) going up on the outside of the house, so that one family may live below, and another above, without going in at the same door; which is the Scots way of living, and which we see in Alnwick and Warkworth, and several other towns.[33]

In the countryside single-storey accommodation was the norm for agricultural labourers. As late as 1841 the Revd W S Gilly found that in Norham single-roomed hovels outnumbered their two-roomed neighbours by six to one. In fact they bore a striking resemblance to the shiels dotting the river banks. Such rudimentary housing was probably already rare in central Berwick before the end of the 18th century, but late 18th- and early 19th-century commentators noted the particular concentration of poorer properties in Tweedmouth and Spittal; they were also to be found in Wallace Green and in the Greenses area of Berwick. Most of those that survive have been amalgamated to provide larger living units. The majority are in Spittal, but they can also be seen in Tweedmouth, for example at 46 and 49 Church Road (Fig 80), and Low Greens. Given the longevity of this building tradition there is no reason to suppose that the surviving examples are especially early; most appear to date from the first half of the 19th century, but a few may be earlier.

By 1850 Berwick's housing problems were coming to a head. In that year a sanitary report to the General Board of Health by the civil engineer Robert Rawlinson drew attention to the lamentable state of Berwick's worst housing and to the consequences, notably endemic typhus and recurrent outbreaks of cholera. Some of the blame was attributed to the influx of Irish labourers – many of them in flight from the desperate poverty resulting from the Potato Famine – who had helped to build the railway. Many families were crowded into the squalid court housing which lay concealed behind the street frontages. Here accommodation was commonly let in 'room-tenements' – bad enough when housing a single family, but rendered still more insanitary by the overcrowding

Figure 80
Single-storey houses at 46 and 49 Church Road,
Tweedmouth – once four separate dwellings – typify the
standard of labourers' accommodation prevalent in the
surrounding countryside and fossilised in the design of
the area's fishing shiels.
[DP065272]

resulting from taking in lodgers. A mixture of actual observation and reports of the incidence of disease and rates of mortality identified Wallace Green, Walkergate and Chapel Street as the unhealthiest parts of the town (Fig 81).

In the years that followed, many of the sanitary report's recommendations were carried into effect (Figs 82 and 83). The public pants, on which poorer people had relied for their water supply, were replaced by piped water derived from augmented sources, banishing the recurrent water shortages of the past. The suggestion that the ramparts be cleared where they confined the churchyard of Holy Trinity, so that the graveyard could be enlarged, was resisted. Instead burials at Holy Trinity Church ceased and large new cemeteries were opened beyond the urban fringe – on Berwick's North Road in 1856 and in 1858 in part of the former King's Quarry on what became Cemetery Lane, Tweedmouth. A new Urban Sanitary Authority was established in 1850, eventually taking possession of the town gaol and court house in Wallace Green in 1892 (Figs 84a and b). The cattle market was removed from its long-established site in Castlegate and from 1886 operated in the now-drained 'Stank' outside the ramparts.

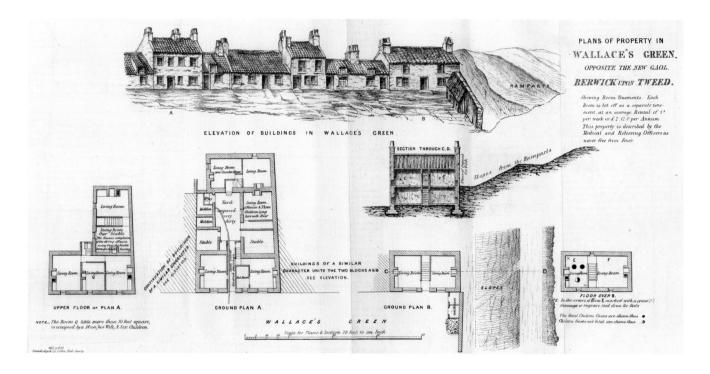

As for the worst housing, Rawlinson had urged that there was 'no remedy … but its removal'.[34] There was, however, a mass of sub-standard housing to deal with and the legal apparatus available to local authorities was still far from adequate, even where the political will existed. Local building by-laws did not forbid new court housing, but they imposed rules concerning room size, lighting, ventilation, drainage, sewerage and the layout of streets, ensuring a gradual improvement, albeit one that was moderated by the standards and expectations prevailing in the wider region. Tenemented housing and small numbers of rooms were tolerated to an extent unusual in other parts of England (though common in Scotland) and led to the widespread adoption of 'cottage tenements' as mooted by Rawlinson.

The commonest type of cottage tenement was a two-storeyed building containing a ground-floor and a first-floor flat, similar to the 'Tyneside flats' built in huge numbers in Newcastle, Gateshead and elsewhere on the Tyne.

Figure 81
Detailed drawings of the worst housing in Wallace Green accompanied Robert Rawlinson's Board of Health report. [Berwick-upon-Tweed Record Office, E26/7]

Figure 82 (above)
The initials of the Berwick-upon-Tweed Local Board
of Health appear on this cast-iron cover for an
inspection trap.
[DP065628]

Figure 83 (right)
Stained glass in the south aisle of Holy Trinity Church
in memory of Dr Alexander Kirkwood (d 1855), one of
Berwick's foremost campaigners for public health.
Kirkwood carried out a detailed investigation into the
sanitary condition of Berwick's population, providing
much of the evidence on which Rawlinson based his
conclusions.
[DP065617]

Most can be recognised from the presence of two or four front entrances, usually side by side, one of which opens directly on to a stair to the first-floor flat (Fig 85). But some have a less formal division between the flats, sharing a single front entrance off which the stair rises. As in Scotland's towns and cities, tenements were not confined to the poorest levels of society; indeed, as an 'improved' form of dwelling they are unlikely to have housed the very poorest. However, those built in Berwick (principally in the Greenses), and more numerously in Tweedmouth and Spittal, were restricted to a relatively narrow social range. Cottage tenements were being built by the 1890s in such streets as Etal Road and Mount Road, Tweedmouth, and Main Street, Spittal, as well as in the Greenses, and it is likely that they replaced much of the earlier single-storey housing by then deemed sub-standard. After the First World War, when the local authority took up the challenge of providing social housing, comparable accommodation remained an important component of the new housing estates, notably in Tweedmouth, where numerous apparently semi-detached houses turn out to be groups of four flats.

Figure 84

a) (below, left) When it was built in 1848–9 the new town gaol and court house attracted some notoriety: critics said that the £8,500 spent building it might more usefully have been spent improving the desperate sanitation of the houses on the opposite side of Wallace Green, subsequently highlighted in Rawlinson's sanitary report. [DP071143]

b) (below, right) In 1892 the building became the headquarters of the Urban Sanitary Authority. [DP065203]

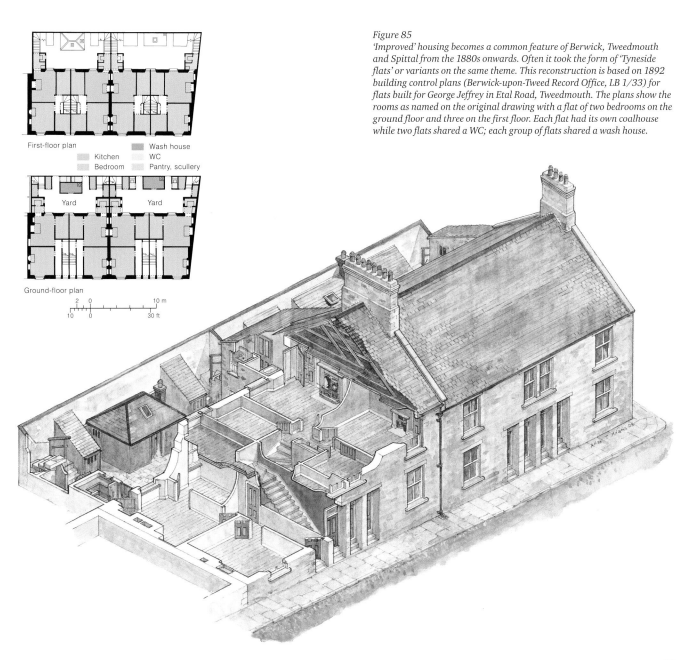

First-floor plan

Kitchen
Bedroom

Wash house
WC
Pantry, scullery

Ground-floor plan

Yard   Yard

2   0   10 m
10   0   30 ft

Figure 85
'Improved' housing becomes a common feature of Berwick, Tweedmouth and Spittal from the 1880s onwards. Often it took the form of 'Tyneside flats' or variants on the same theme. This reconstruction is based on 1892 building control plans (Berwick-upon-Tweed Record Office, LB 1/33) for flats built for George Jeffrey in Etal Road, Tweedmouth. The plans show the rooms as named on the original drawing with a flat of two bedrooms on the ground floor and three on the first floor. Each flat had its own coalhouse while two flats shared a WC; each group of flats shared a wash house.

Figure 86 (left)
The building housing the police station, court house and police court in Church Street was designed by R Burns Dick.
[DP065171]

Figure 87 (right)
Spittal's police station was this domestic-looking building, described in the 1912 designs as a Lock-up and Constable's Quarters.
[Berwick-upon-Tweed Record Office, Building Control Plans, Box 3]

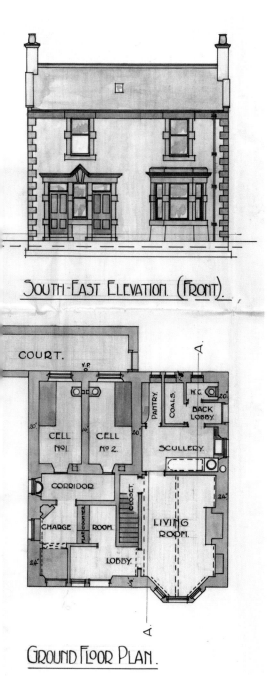

SOUTH-EAST ELEVATION (FRONT).

GROUND FLOOR PLAN.

Housing reform was paralleled by the restructuring of essential services. A new building housing a police station, court house and police court, designed by R Burns Dick, opened on Church Street in 1900 (Fig 86), and Spittal's once notoriously rowdy populace was placed under the watchful eye of a constable installed in a new police house on Commercial Road (Fig 87). The 1870 Education Act had opened the door to publicly funded education administered by School Boards, but it was not until 1903 (under the revised terms of the 1902 Education Act) that Berwick opened its first Council School, the Infants' School in High Greens, designed by J Landell Nicholson and Fred E Dotchin of Newcastle. Others quickly followed: Tweedmouth Council School (now Tweedmouth West First School), Osborne Road, in 1904 and Spittal Council School (now Spittal Community School), Main Street, in 1908. Perhaps observing a similar improving spirit, the brewers of Berwick and Tweedmouth embarked on a campaign of rebuilding, as a result of which numerous Berwick pubs received facelifts in the years immediately before the First World War.

Even after these achievements much poor-quality housing remained. The elimination of this housing required the greater powers awarded to local authorities under the 1919 Housing Act, which enabled them to acquire land and build council houses with financial assistance from the state. The houses and flats of the Borough Housing Scheme, erected in Tweedmouth from 1921 on former agricultural land and supplemented by the nearly contemporary philanthropic housing project, Askew Crescent (1925–8) on Billendean Road, gave the town space to breathe, bringing light and air into the most densely built-up quarters whilst affording better living conditions for those rehoused. As the Tweedmouth estate grew it accommodated another initiative designed to ease the rapidly increasing flow of motor traffic on the Great North Road. The building of the Royal Tweed Bridge was accompanied by the demolition of much of Golden Square, a run-down court, which had once been a vibrant centre of Presbyterian worship off Marygate. On the Tweedmouth side a new approach, named Prince Edward Road after the future Edward VIII, who opened the bridge in 1928, cut through the knot of small streets and houses forming Knowe Head at the top of Main Street and Kiln Hill. The incongruity between the clean, broad lines of the new road and the irregular jumble of houses and narrow streets through which it passes is still palpable.

6

Leisurely pursuits

The working lives of past centuries are typically easier to document than the pursuits people turned to in their leisure hours. Employment, trades and professions defined people: they were used to confirm identities in legal documents and were listed extensively in commercial directories; many trades evolved buildings with particular characteristics that remain clearly identifiable today, or employed tools and raw materials that were enumerated in probate inventories; and the wealth that accrued can be judged not only from probate and taxation records but from the scale and elaboration of surviving houses. By contrast many leisure activities – whether concealed within the domestic sphere, conducted in the open air, or carried on in buildings primarily serving other purposes – go largely unrecorded. Yet if work defines lives legally and economically, leisure is perhaps a truer reflection of a society's deeper yearnings and over time these found growing expression in the urban environment.

Not all leisure activities took place entirely outside the economic sphere. The many inns and taverns met a local, recreational need in addition to serving travellers and acting as a focal point for the local carriers' networks linking Berwick with neighbouring towns and villages. In 1806 James Good's *Directory* identified 66 public houses in Berwick, a further 9 in Tweedmouth and 5 in Spittal. Berwick's pubs were distributed quite widely around the town's main streets, but there were particular concentrations in Hide Hill (14) and Marygate (11), where markets generated extra custom. It is striking, too, that Parade, which now has no pubs at all, had 8 in 1806, clearly ministering to the needs of the Barracks. The larger establishments, especially the principal inns (the King's Arms on Hide Hill, the Red Lion on Marygate and the Hen and Chickens on Sandgate), offered a wider range of services, including large rooms capable of accommodating assemblies at the King's Arms and the Red Lion. Lancelot Turner, the publican of the Barley Mow in Marygate, catered for different tastes by keeping a billiard table.[35] On a more substantial scale, a theatre – complete with gallery, pit and boxes, and engaging the services of a Newcastle scene-painter – was established behind the King's Arms in about 1798 by Stephen Kemble. Theatrical productions coincided with the July horse races at Lamberton, just over the border in Scotland.[36]

In a similar vein the primary purpose of Berwick's various markets, its annual cattle and horse fair in Castlegate, and its two annual hiring fairs for agricultural labour was the trading of goods or services, but they must also

Figure 88
Greenses Haven from the clifftop shelter.
[DP065626]

have been accompanied by entertainments and other diversions. The annual three-day Easter Walls Fair of the early 19th century, when 'the whole ramparts and parade are so crowded, that you would really imagine the whole inhabitants of the town are turned out to view one another',[37] blended commercial and social interests seamlessly. The annual Tweedmouth Feast seems to have been a more purely convivial event, though closely linked to daily life since each family was expected to furnish a dish of baked salmon. Spittal had a similar tradition.

The surrounding coast and countryside, including Greenses Haven (Fig 88), the nearby Magdalene Fields and the riverside paths linking the many shiels, must at all times have attracted those in search of fresh air, tranquillity and intimacy. The more formal fashion for promenading, which afforded both healthful exercise and an occasion for polite conversation, found an outlet on the ramparts, especially as their military significance dwindled (Fig 89). In 1816, to alleviate the impact of the slump that followed the end of the Napoleonic Wars, employment was provided on the construction of both Pier Road (Fig 90), leading to the newly completed pier and lighthouse, and New Road, extending from Love Lane to Carlin Brae. Both served, in the words of Thomas Johnstone, to 'unite pleasure with utility', providing additional riverside promenades.[38]

Figure 89
An engraving of the ramparts in use as a public promenade.
[Berwick-upon-Tweed Record Office, Fuller 1799, facing p 183]

Figure 90
Pier Road, built as a remedy for unemployment in the aftermath of the Napoleonic Wars, formed a popular coastal promenade extending as far as the lighthouse. Later the existence of the road attracted industrial, and then residential development, as well as quarters for soldiers and coastguard officers.
[DP065234]

The growth of cultural institutions was arguably hindered by the town's unusual constitution, which discouraged patronage by the landed aristocracy (*see* p 6), and by a characteristic preoccupation with business affairs among the commercial elite. But Berwick was not culturally benighted, as the succession of home-grown historians from the cultivated Dr Fuller onwards confirms. The Berwick Subscription Library, established in Bridge Street in 1811, was perhaps the town's first purpose-built institution of this sort. The Subscription Reading Room, Billiard Room and Bowling Green in Palace Green followed before 1843 and a Mechanics' Institution and News Room in Marygate served the artisan community from 1850. One of Berwick's most distinguished achievements in the cultural sphere was the 1831 formation of the Berwickshire Naturalists' Club, one of the earliest provincial natural history societies (Fig 91). Its collection became the nucleus of the Berwick Borough Museum, founded in 1867; the museum opened in new premises (as the Berwick Institution & Reading Room, 32 Marygate) in 1882.

Organised sport, which in the 19th century was increasingly promoted as a way of inculcating the physical and mental aptitudes deemed beneficial for empire-building, also made its mark in the mid-19th century. A cricket ground was in use on Magdalene Fields by the 1850s and in 1869 Berwick Amateur Rowing Club was established; still flourishing today, its wooden boathouse, extended in 1893, stands on New Road (Fig 92). Berwick Rangers Football Club traces its origins to 1881, though it did not move to its present Shielfield Park ground in Tweedmouth until 1954. Famously, it competes not in the English but in the Scottish Football League.

The growth of the resort

Spittal's emergence as both a spa and a seaside resort is the more striking because it proceeded alongside the development of Spittal Point for a variety of large-scale industrial enterprises and despite the unenviable reputation of Spittal's housing. In 1799 Fuller warned that the 'intolerably bad' condition of most of Spittal's houses and the resulting prevalence of disease made it 'but ill suited to the great number of people who resort to it in summer for the mineral water as well as for sea bathing'.[39] Nevertheless, claimed Good, the spa 'collects many respectable families from the country' and 'has made many cures among the poor'.[40] The spa water, rich in iron and sulphur, emerges near the foot of Spittal Banks close to what is now Main Street, but well to the south-east of the early settlement (Fig 93). Something approaching the formality of a grassy square developed around and below the spring, and a number of houses alongside – probably including Spa Well House – provided lodgings, though in the summer demand for lodgings might outstrip supply. A vivid impression of the up-and-coming resort, informal but apparently thriving, is given by John Dixon Evans' engraved *View of Berwick upon Tweed, its Suburbs, and Bay*. Published in 1829, it shows bathing machines and elegantly attired

Figure 91 (top)
George Johnston's house in Woolmarket. In 1832 Johnston (1797–1855), a doctor and naturalist, helped to found the Berwickshire Naturalists' Club, one of the earliest provincial learned societies. [DP071139]

Figure 92 (above)
The timber boathouse of Berwick Amateur Rowing Club. [DP071108]

Figure 93 (right)
Before the end of the 18th century Spittal Spa was attracting visitors, many of whom wished to lodge in the vicinity. The gentle formality of the spa's setting later proved attractive for siting Spittal's war memorial. [DP065639]

holidaymakers sharing the foreshore with salmon fishermen and the horse-drawn coal wagons of the Berwick Pier Railway (Fig 94).

    The development of the resort seems to have gathered pace during the 1830s and by 1837 the name 'Spittal New Town' was applied to the area bordering the southern end of Main Street (Fig 95). But the label 'New Town' was short-lived (it does not appear after the 1850s); new building was far from systematic and the result has a puzzling look. The houses built between about 1830 and 1850 are mostly modest villas (frequently named 'cottages', as was the fashion). A number – such as Terrace Cottage (174 Main Street) and Rose Bank Cottage, perched near the top of the brae on Cow Road – turn squarely towards the sea and capitalise on a degree of elevation; Spa Well Terrace, offering taller, more compact accommodation, does the same. But the majority of the houses, though built on the seaward side of the road, face inland (Fig 96), some of them having long front gardens but only a small yard on the seaward side. The names of Brighton House (now St John's Vicarage) and Bay View (107 Main Street), both of which face inland, are almost incongruous.

Figure 94
Detail from View of Berwick upon Tweed, its Suburbs, and Bay. Designed in 1822, when His Majesty King George the IVth was detained in the Bay on his tour to Edinburgh, *showing the Berwick Pier Railway, salmon fishermen and sea-bathers.*
[Painted by J D Evans, engraved by R Scott and published by R Good in 1829; by permission of Berwick-upon-Tweed Corporation (Freemen) Trustees, DP065677]

A fastidious shunning of the workaday sights and sounds of the Berwick Pier Railway, which curtailed the building plots on this side of the road and was still operational when at least some of these houses were being built, is perhaps partly responsible (the original track was lifted between 1852 and 1860, and the colliery extension was joined to the main line railway). The first occupants of many of these villas remain to be discovered. Some were adopted by local people seeking a suburban lifestyle: Bay View was home in 1855 to John Wilson, an iron merchant whose family business was based in Bridge Street, Berwick. But others will have been rented to holidaymakers, while many operated as lodging houses.

Figure 95
Spittal as depicted on the 1837 Plan of Berwick Harbour, *with the nascent resort labelled 'Spittal New Town'.*
[Berwick-upon-Tweed Museum & Art Gallery, DP065592]

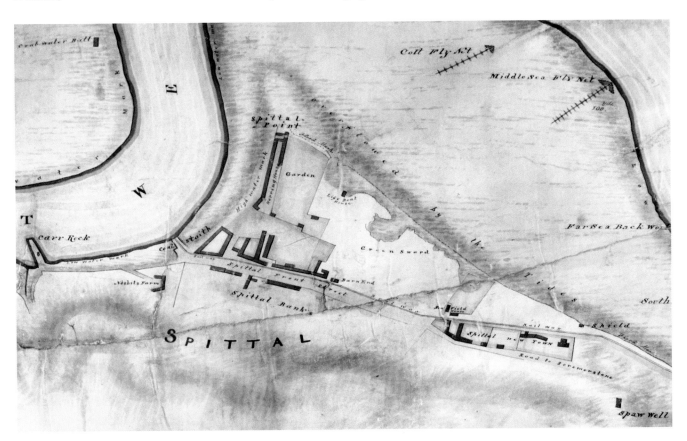

Spittal New Town, with its substantial houses mostly set amid generous wooded gardens, is a world away from both the tangle of small fishermen's houses, curing sheds, shops and pubs at the opposite end of Spittal and the industrial quarter of Spittal Point. They were to remain largely separate worlds, despite being under each other's noses. The resort expanded slowly southwards till it reached the limit imposed by the cliffs approaching Huds Head. The main exception to this trend was the building – in or shortly after 1897 for the Boston family – of St Helen's Terrace, 15 houses boldly fronting the sea only a stone's throw from Spittal's gasworks. With uninterrupted sea views, no fewer than 8 of these houses offered rooms to let on the eve of the First World War. The spot had no doubt become more attractive with the demise of Guthrie's iron foundry to its rear and with the provision of Spittal's first parish church, St John the Evangelist (consecrated 1871), on Main Street near the point where the fishing village and resort met. But Spittal remained a quiet resort with few amusements or other novelties. At the beginning of the 20th century it had a promenade, a bandstand, a bowling green and a tennis

Figure 96 (above)
Balmoral House, a modest mid-19th-century seaside villa, turns its back on the sea.
[DP065728]

Figure 97 (left)
Many a holidaymaker in Spittal or Berwick will have sampled Berwick Cockles, a boiled sweet peculiar to the town.
[DP065143]

court; in 1922 the local ice-cream manufacturers Forte Brothers built the earliest part of the present refreshment room. Today on a summer's day it remains popular with families and beachcombers who appreciate its spacious beach and relaxed atmosphere.

Berwick, too, developed a minor resort function (Fig 97). Visitors came for its increasingly admired townscape, its sea and river views, and its convenience as a base for touring the countryside. Greenses Haven (*see* Fig 88), once the preserve of fishermen and quarrymen, became a popular beach. A 'Bathing Hole' – an apparently natural formation of the rocky foreshore – was noted on the Ordnance Survey map as early as 1857 and by the 1920s two concrete-walled pools, one for men and one for women, were in use, replenished by each incoming tide (Fig 98). These must have been heavily used during the brief life of the adjacent clifftop army camp, which after the Second World War was adapted to serve as a holiday camp, attracting mainly Scottish holidaymakers (*see* Fig 36). The artist L S Lowry (1887–1976) was a frequent

Figure 98 (below)
One of Berwick's two former sea-water bathing pools at Greenses Haven, as depicted on a 1960s postcard. Huts belonging to the wartime army camp remain on the clifftop.
[AFL03/Lilywhite/BTC3]

visitor to Berwick in the post-war years and among the features he selected to paint was the simple shelter erected near the landward end of the pier.

Facilities in the town centre primarily served a local audience, though they offered wet-weather attractions for holidaymakers. Berwick did not acquire a purpose-built theatre until the Maltings Arts Centre opened in 1990, though plays and other entertainments were sometimes staged in the Corn Exchange, opened in 1858 (Fig 99). But when Charles Dickens, on his 1861 reading tour, learnt that he was to perform in 'An immense Corn Exchange, made of glass and iron, round, dome-topp'd, lofty, utterly absurd for any such purpose, and full of thundering echoes', he promptly insisted on reverting to the 'primitive accommodation' (as it was now viewed) of the theatre behind the King's Arms.[41] Other additions to Berwick's attractions followed. In 1903 the Magdalene Fields Golf Club was established with a 9-hole clifftop course, later extended to 18 holes. Berwick's first cinema was the Playhouse, an austere pedimented brick shed in Sandgate that opened in 1912 in the wake of

Figure 99
Berwick's Corn Exchange, opened in 1858, also served as a venue for entertainments.
[DP056352]

Figure 100
Berwick's first cinema, the Playhouse, opened in 1912.
[DP065170]

the safety-conscious Cinematograph Act of 1909 and closed as recently as 2005 (Fig 100). It was joined in 1927 by the classical Berwick Theatre (now a bingo club) on Hide Hill, designed by the Southport architect Albert Schofield.

Easy access to the coast and countryside made public parks a less urgent need than in many larger towns and cities, but it was the latter that shaped expectations and by the late 19th century few towns could afford to be without some public green space. Castle Vale Park occupies the steeply sloping valley of Berwick's principal stream, which ceased to be harnessed for water power when the Tappee Pond was drained and infilled to create the sidings and engine sheds just north of Castle Bridge. Early in the 20th century a portion of this flat land was used to create a curling pond, while the steep-sided valley below the bridge was fashioned into a municipal park connected by footpaths to the riverside. Here the steep slopes resist the hand of man, who has clothed them with paths and flower beds without ever obliterating the ancient landscape from which the town emerged.

7

Safeguarding Berwick's past for the future

Attitudes to the past have changed dramatically over the past two centuries: as a nation we view the historic environment more inclusively, valuing not just the great stone circles, cathedrals and castles of our ancient past, but our 'minor' and more recent heritage as well, and increasingly the wider historic landscapes of which they form part (Fig 101). In so doing we reflect a growing recognition of the positive contribution that the historic environment makes to our quality of life.

Berwick has been proud of its antiquity for a long time. But it entered the 19th century with its Elizabethan ramparts – never tested in war – essentially intact and, like most walled towns, found such a substantial necklace restrictive, especially where the gates choked traffic along the Great North Road. In 1806 James Good noted: 'The greatest evil that attends this town is the narrow passages or entrances, both from the English and Scotch gates.'[42] By this time the Shore Gate had already been altered (in 1760), to improve access to the Quay. In a further attempt to ease congestion the Scotch Gate was altered in 1815 and the Main Guard, which had formed a notable obstruction in Marygate and had latterly suffered the indignity of serving as a woolcomber's warehouse, was dismantled. Although contemporaries seem to have agreed that there was no practical benefit to be derived from the now obsolete defences, there was clearly much affection for them as emblems of the town's distinguished, if turbulent, past and as proof of its antiquity. James Graham (presumably the Marygate resident variously described as a twine-spinner and starch-maker in 1806[43] and as a grocer and flax-dresser in 1811)[44] led a successful campaign to save the Main Guard, which was re-erected in a substantially altered form in Palace Street (Fig 102). But if this was a victory snatched from the jaws of progress it was a small one. Ness Gate was punched through the ramparts about 1810 to provide more convenient access to the new pier, then being built. The English Gate, defending the approach from London across Berwick Bridge, was removed in 1825 (Fig 103; *see also* Fig 25) and Scotch Gate was altered again in 1858. The Cow Port, which led nowhere but the Magdalene Fields and the fishing boat havens beneath the cliff, is thus the only gate to retain its 16th-century form.

Major instances of destruction or radical alteration, such as those affecting the town gates and the castle, are understandably eye-catching but can distract attention from the more pervasive effects of gradual change. Over a long

Figure 101
The view from the roof of the Town Hall, looking south down Hide Hill, with parts of Spittal and Tweedmouth in the distance. The sinuous curve of the street frontage hints at the forces shaping the early town; the steeply pitched upstanding gable on Forte's Restaurant points to the phased evolution of the town's built fabric; and the variations of materials – pantile and slate roofs, stone and rendered walls – show how complex an artefact is a town like Berwick.
[DP071090]

Figure 102
The Main Guard as rebuilt in Palace Street.
[DP071140]

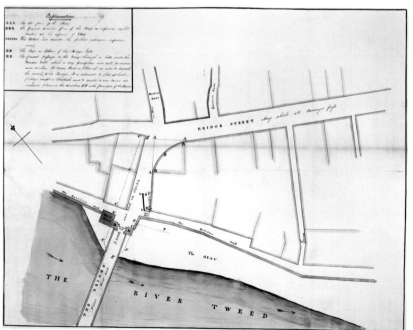

Figure 103
During the 1820s the English Gate and its environs were altered substantially, as this plan, prepared in 1823, shows. One awkward street corner had already been replaced with an easier curved profile and the roadway was to be adjusted in order to lessen the steepness of the ascent to Berwick Bridge. Shortly afterwards, in 1825, the gate defending the bridge was removed.
[The National Archives, MPH 1/983/2]

Figure 104
During the 20th century, as the new estates spread, spare capacity in the housing stock allowed inferior housing to be eradicated. Single-storey housing, mostly dating from before 1850, was particularly targeted. Here in Church Road, Tweedmouth, only vestiges of the two gables indicate the nature of what the garages have replaced. [DP065268]

period Berwick was transformed by essentially benign policies of local administration, such as those which saw cramped and unsanitary housing eradicated or drastically thinned (Fig 104) and its replacement first by privately built cottage flats (Fig 105) and, after the First World War, mostly by local authority housing. Equally dramatic consequences have sometimes resulted from innocuous but pervasive economic and social trends. The arrival of the railway, for example, encouraged an incipient trend among better-off residents seeking a more spacious and private lifestyle on the outskirts of the town. The earliest villas on Castle Terrace actually pre-date the railway's arrival, but proliferated from the 1840s – powerfully reinforced by the proximity of the railway station – to become Berwick's principal villa grouping. Other villas were scattered around the edge of Tweedmouth. These were the substantial houses of merchants, industrialists and professional people in the main. However, from the beginning of the 20th century people of more moderate means increasingly removed themselves from Berwick's town centre, first to developments like the ample terraced houses of Northumberland Avenue, Warkworth Terrace and Percy Terrace and, in the 1930s, to the spreading estates of semi-detached houses on both sides of North Road and south of Billendean Road in Spittal. Such a trend, in a period when outward migration resulted in a static or declining population, progressively weakened demand for residential properties in the town, and by the 1960s some of Berwick's finest 18th- and 19th-century houses were in a perilous state. Bringing so many of these houses back from the brink over the ensuing decades was a major achievement (Fig 106).

Figure 105 (left)
After the First World War hundreds of new homes were built on former agricultural land. The recently refurbished Askew Crescent was built by the local Askew family to commemorate the visit of Edward Prince of Wales when he opened the Royal Tweed Bridge in 1928. [DP065645]

Figure 106 (below)
The painter L S Lowry once considered buying Lions House (shown here on the left) but abandoned his plans when he became aware of its poor condition; by the early 1970s it was derelict. The house and the 1749 magazine (shown here on the right), restored by English Heritage, make vital contributions to the coherence and public appreciation of the historic environment. [DP071142]

Renewed development pressure in the mid-2000s, mainly for new apartments as a result of an increased demand for second homes, led to the proposed redevelopment of some critical sites within the town (Fig 107). The need for an overall strategy, based on a sound understanding of the character of the area, culminated in a new initiative which was to consider the physical, economic and social regeneration of the town. Berwick's Future is a partnership of local and regional organisations (Berwick-upon-Tweed Borough Council, Berwick-upon Tweed Town Council, Berwick Community Trust, English Heritage, Government Office for the North East, Northumberland County Council, Northumberland Strategic Partnership, One NorthEast and the Local Strategic Partnership) dedicated to planning a successful future for the town and delivering the vision of Berwick as 'a competitive, distinctive and well-connected border town that is enterprising, ambitious and inclusive'.[45] English Heritage has been a key partner since the project's inception in 2005.

Berwick is entering a period of opportunity and change. Statistical projections in 2005 suggested that without concerted action the town will struggle to retain its younger population, to generate employment outside the seasonal tourist industry, to provide affordable housing for its residents and to compete with other retail centres. Berwick's Future Regeneration Strategy (produced by consultants Urban Initiatives in 2008) sets out a number of key challenges if the town is to hold its own in the 21st century: building on and enhancing its core assets in order to retain and attract population, developing the town's role as a focus for sustainable communities and improving its performance as a market centre.

How does Berwick achieve this? The Regeneration Strategy, expanding on the initial Vision and Development Framework (produced by a consultant team from Gillespies in 2006), proposes the creation of a polycentric urban structure embracing Berwick, Tweedmouth and Spittal. Instead of the town centre being constrained by the fortifications, town centre functions could expand beyond their traditional focus to provide further development opportunities. This proposal could be seen to follow the historic pattern of growth in the town whereby industrial, and later residential, growth has been accommodated disproportionately in Tweedmouth and Spittal. Resolving the issues of traffic management and car parking will be essential – a common problem for walled towns across Europe (Fig 108). At the same time, a culture change is needed to

Figure 107
A series of derelict industrial buildings on Spittal Point were demolished in 2005, leaving just the chimney as a reminder of their previous uses.
[DP071141]

persuade people that a polycentric Berwick is a *walkable* town and that the river is not the dividing line it has been in the past. A team from Colin Buchanan & Partners was commissioned by the Berwick's Future partnership to produce the *Berwick-upon-Tweed Traffic Management and Parking Strategy* to consider in detail the problems of getting to and around the town, to address comprehensively the issue of car parking and to propose solutions promoting the wider strategy while respecting the context of the historic town.

Alongside the Berwick's Future initiative the regional development agency, One NorthEast, is carrying forward its market towns programme and has commissioned a number of Tourism Destination Management Plans for Northumberland towns, including Berwick. The Berwick plan covers the period from 2008 to 2018 and aims to develop tourism potential and strengthen its identity as a walled border town. The plan sets out clear objectives and a strategy for achieving the vision which includes making the fortifications and other heritage of the town a 'destination priority'.[46] The Barracks site, within the guardianship of English Heritage, has been highlighted in both the Regeneration Strategy and the Tourism Destination Management Plan as being a key project for further development as a tourist

Figure 108
The Elizabethan fortifications between Cumberland Bastion and Brass Bastion. This significant open space (originally the moat or 'Stank') outside the ramparts and thus an integral part of the historic defences is at risk from proposals for additional car parking for the town. Whilst parking is a critical issue for the town, cluttering the fortifications with cars would detract from the very features that attract people to the town. [DP071110]

destination in the area. Work is ongoing to develop this idea in consultation with partners in the town, the first step of which has been to commission a Conservation Statement to set out the significance of various elements of the site and identify levels of acceptable change to the buildings.

As all of these initiatives progress, how will the historic environment fare and where will conservation policy fit in as the town continues to evolve? Conservation is about the management, not the prevention, of change (Fig 109). This book has set out how the town has developed over the centuries and how it has evolved in response to the landscape, to changing economic circumstances and, particularly significant for Berwick, to its border location. The imprint of history – still legible in its buildings and townscapes, in its rich

Figure 109
The quayside, Berwick. Once a thriving and bustling industrial area, it is now partly used for car parking whilst the remainder is largely unkempt open space. The ability to see the Quay Walls in their entirety is a relatively recent phenomenon and one which some would wish to retain. However, the quayside has enormous potential to provide a destination for visitors and locals alike and to reinvigorate this part of the town. Could contemporary design enrich this setting? [NMR 20687/54]

archival collection or concealed beneath the ground but still shaping what we see – makes Berwick the fascinating and much-loved place that it is today. Its historic environment is a unique resource and one which forms the basis of the Berwick's Future Regeneration Strategy. It is vital that the project achieves a balance between growth and development on the one hand and, on the other, maintaining those special qualities that make the town an attractive place to live and work in and to visit.

The Regeneration Strategy highlights the 'uniqueness of Berwick' and stresses the three-dimensional character of the town: the valley and coastal topography and the layering of water, fortified walls and 'dancing' roofscape. Tweedmouth and Spittal also have distinctive character that needs to be understood and respected when new development is considered. The Rapid Character Assessment produced by English Heritage in 2005, amplified by two Conservation Area Character Appraisals for Berwick and Tweedmouth produced by the North of England Civic Trust in 2007–8 with extensive community involvement, provides an analysis of what makes particular areas distinctive. These documents are invaluable tools in the design process and should help to steer new developments towards appropriate locations and forms so that they add a new layer of significance to the town's history as well as advancing the Regeneration Strategy's objectives.

The Regeneration Strategy addresses broad, strategic issues but other measures are required to deal with more localised problems. One effect of a struggling economy has been reduced pressure to alter or redevelop buildings, but it has also meant that it has been difficult for building owners to maintain buildings adequately. Heavily overgrown gutters and blocked downpipes are a common feature of the town and the resulting water penetration causes long-term damage. Heritage Economic Regeneration Schemes (partnership grant schemes funded by English Heritage and Berwick-upon-Tweed Borough Council) in Berwick, Tweedmouth and Spittal in the early part of the present decade have encouraged the repair of historic buildings, but more help is needed to tackle this issue and to advise building owners of the importance of maintenance.

Good management of the historic environment depends upon sound understanding of its significance and the research carried out in the preparation of this book will underpin the protection of buildings within the town as a

Figure 110
Careful investigation of historic buildings, especially in advance of planned change, will reveal many aspects of the town's past. Here two different historic wallpapers are revealed inside a cupboard. The 'arch and pillar' design of the lower wallpaper belongs to a well-known 18th-century type, but many historic wallpapers have not survived and even fragmentary survivals may be significant.
[DP065397]

whole. At the time of writing the timetable for new Heritage Protection legislation is uncertain but there is a clear trend towards consideration of the historic environment as a coherent whole rather than as a collection of disjointed assets. The current register of listed buildings for Berwick is more than 35 years old and reflects the values prevalent in the early 1970s, omitting a number of buildings now considered to be nationally significant.

The research has also involved the local community and an important part of English Heritage's work has been to facilitate the local Berwick Building Recording Group with the aim of creating local capacity to research and record historic buildings. The group began in 2007 and, with assistance from English Heritage, continues to survey and research buildings within the town. Concurrently, a project was initiated by Berwick-upon-Tweed Borough Council to promote the use of the borough archives and provide training in archival research. Berwick is fortunate to have this resource located within the town.

Future architectural and archaeological research will need to probe more deeply Berwick's pre-18th-century fabric, most of which lies concealed behind later refrontings or buried beneath the ground, but there are many other avenues for research (Fig 110). The investigation of historic buildings and the

Figure 111 (left)
Tweedmouth and Spittal residents have long valued the partly wooded area known as the Goody Patchy and the grass strip adjoining Dock Road. Both are, in their present form, relatively recent creations: the Goody Patchy was bare of trees as late as the 1940s and the grassy sward covers the course of the old Tweed Dock Branch Railway, itself laid down on land reclaimed from the estuary. But they have amenity value for walkers, they help preserve the separate identities of Tweedmouth and Spittal, and they diversify views across the Tweed.
[NMR 20687/52]

identification and – where appropriate – excavation of archaeological remains are mutually informative approaches, which have the potential to clarify much that is currently obscure in Berwick's past as well as to provide a firm evidential basis for informed decision-making in the planning process. In the past emphasis has been placed on the significance of the walled town, its fortifications and military history, but less attention has been devoted to the rich inheritance of domestic, institutional and industrial buildings, to the outlying settlements of Tweedmouth and Spittal, and to the particular value of open spaces (Fig 111). English Heritage hopes that by building a deeper understanding of the town's buildings, streets and open spaces, a clearer sense will emerge of their significance for the local community (Fig 112). Greater understanding generates an increased willingness to care for the historic environment and encourages healthy engagement with the process of managing change. If Berwick, Tweedmouth and Spittal are to flourish, the careful management of change must be an integral part of the strategy for the future.

Figure 112 (right)
Members of Berwick Building Recording Group recording the former Subscription Reading Room and Billard Room on Palace Green.
[DP071258]

Notes

1 Pevsner 1957, 88

2 William Whellan & Co 1855, 962–4

3 Gough's 1806 edn of Camden 1607, 498

4 Morgan 1992, 77

5 Good 1806, 157

6 *Kelly's Directory* 1914, 3

7 Fuller 1799, 476

8 Brenchley 1997, 99–101

9 Fuller 1799, 357

10 BL Cotton MS Augustus I.ii.14

11 Fuller 1799, 388

12 Fuller 1799, 182

13 Fuller 1799, 409–10

14 Jorvin 1672, quoted in Fuller 1799, 42

15 Anon 1818, 35–7

16 Colvin 1982, 655

17 *The Berwick Journal* 28 Oct 1886

18 Brenchley 1997, 5, 278

19 Bates 1891, 6

20 Colvin 1975, 232n

21 White 1859, 285

22 Gomme 1896, 257

23 Fuller 1799, 424

24 Good 1806, 51–7

25 *Berwick Advertiser* 19 Oct 1838

26 Barfoot and Wilkes 1793–8, 283

27 Good 1806, 153

28 Good 1806, 155

29 Good 1806, 6, 154–5

30 Fuller 1799, 363–4

31 Good 1806, 153–4

32 Priestley 1969, 59–60

33 Defoe 1974, 284

34 Rawlinson 1850, 18

35 Good 1806, 50

36 Good 1806, 100

37 Good 1806, 101

38 Johnstone 1817, 131–3

39 Fuller 1799, 464

40 Good 1806, 155

41 Forster 1966, 241–2

42 Good 1806, 178

43 Good 1806, 50

44 *Holden's Annual Directory for 1811, Vol II* 1811

45 Gillespies *et al* 2006 *The Future of Berwick: A Vision and Development Framework*, 3

46 Miller Consulting with Alison Caffyn April 2008 *Destination Plan for Berwick-upon-Tweed*

References and further reading

Anon 1818 *North of England and Scotland in MDCCIV*. Edinburgh: William Blackwood

Anon 1956 *A Salmon Saga: The story of the Berwick Salmon Fisheries Company Limited 1856–1956*. London: Harley Publishing Co Ltd

Barfoot, P and Wilkes, J (eds) 1793–8 *The Universal British Directory 1793–1798, Vol II*. London: The Patentees at the British Directory Office (facsim edn Michael Winton 1993)

Bates, C J 1891 *Border Holds of Northumberland*. London and Newcastle upon Tyne: Society of Antiquaries

Bowes, E 1998 *Lowry in Berwick*.

Brenchley, D 1997 *A Place by Itself: Berwick-upon-Tweed in the eighteenth century*. Berwick-upon-Tweed: Berwick-upon-Tweed Civic Society

Clifton-Taylor, A 1985 *Six More English Towns*. London: BBC

Colvin, H (ed) 1975 *The History of the King's Works, Vol III: 1485–1660 (Part 1)*. London: HMSO

Colvin, H (ed) 1982 *The History of the King's Works, Vol IV: 1485–1660 (Part 2)*. London: HMSO

Cowe, F M 1998 *Berwick upon Tweed: A short historical guide*, rev edn. Berwick-upon-Tweed: J D Cowe

Cullen, M 2005 *Early Victorian Spittal (1837–1864)*. [Berwick-upon-Tweed]: Michael Cullen

Cullen, M 2006 *Later Victorian Spittal*. [Berwick-upon-Tweed]: Michael Cullen

Defoe, D 1974 *A Tour Through the Whole Island of Great Britain, Vol II*. London: J M Dent

Forster, J 1966 *The Life of Charles Dickens, Vol II*. London: J M Dent & Sons

Fuller, J 1799 *The History of Berwick upon Tweed, including a short account of the villages of Tweedmouth and Spittal, &c* (facsim edn F Graham 1973)

Gilly, W S 1841 *The Peasantry of the Border: An appeal in their behalf* (facsim edn Square Edge Books 2001)

Gomme, G L (ed) 1896 *Topographical History of Norfolk, Northamptonshire, and Northumberland: A classified collection of the chief contents of 'The Gentleman's Magazine' from 1731–1868*. London: Elliot Stock

Good, J 1806 *A Directory and Concise History of Berwick-upon-Tweed ….* Berwick-upon-Tweed: W Lockhead (http://rgcairns.orpheusweb.co.uk/DirectoryContents.html)

Gough, R 1806 edn of Camden, W 1607 *Britannia, Vol III*. London: John Stockdale

Green, C G W 2001 *The Arts in Berwick: A short cultural history*. Berwick-upon-Tweed: Berwick-upon-Tweed Civic Society

Grove, D 1999 *Berwick Barracks and Fortifications*. London: English Heritage

Hewlings, R 1993 'Hawksmoor's brave designs for the police', *in* Bold, J and Chaney, E (eds), *English Architecture, Public and Private: Essays for Kerry Downes*. London: Hambledon Press, 215–29

Holden's Annual Directory for 1811, Vol II 1811 London: W Holden (facsim edn Michael Winton 1996)

Johnstone, T 1817 *The History of Berwick-upon-Tweed and its vicinity, to which is added, a correct copy of the charter granted to that borough* (facsim edn Berwick-upon-Tweed History Society 2004)

Kelly's Directory of Northumberland 1914 London: Kelly's Directories Ltd

Lamont-Brown, R 1988 *The Life and Times of Berwick-upon-Tweed*. Edinburgh: John Donald

Linsley, S 2005 *Ports and Harbours of Northumberland*. Stroud: Tempus

Marlow, J 2000 *Berwick-upon-Tweed: An archaeological assessment* (draft Extensive Urban Survey for English Heritage)

Morgan, K (ed) 1992 *An American Quaker in the British Isles: The travel journals of Jabez Maud Fisher, 1775–1779*. Oxford: Oxford University Press

Pennant, T 1769 *British Zoology, Vol III*. Chester: Benjamin White, 241–5

Pevsner, N 1957 *The Buildings of England: Northumberland*. Harmondsworth: Penguin

Pevsner, N (Grundy, J *et al*) 1992 *The Buildings of England: Northumberland*, 2 edn. London: Penguin

Pigney, J (ed) 2005 *Putting Bondington on the Map: Berwick and its lost northern suburb*. Berwick-upon-Tweed: The Steering Group of Bondington Project

Priestley, J 1969 *Priestley's Navigable Rivers and Canals* (facsim edn with new introduction by C Hadfield). Newton Abbot: David & Charles

Rawlinson, R 1850 *Report to the General Board of Health on a Preliminary Enquiry into the Sewerage, Drainage, and Supply of Water, and the Sanitary Condition of the Inhabitants of the Parish of Berwick-upon-Tweed*. London: W Clowes & Son

Scott, J 1888 *Berwick-upon-Tweed: The history of the town and guild*. London: E Stock

Sheldon, F 1849 *History of Berwick-upon-Tweed*. Edinburgh: Adam and Charles Black

Strang, C A 1994 *Borders and Berwick: An illustrated architectural guide to the Scottish Borders and Tweed Valley*. Edinburgh: Rutland Press

Summerson, H 1995 'From border stronghold to railway station: The fortunes of Berwick Castle 1560–1850'. *Archaeologia Aeliana 5* ser **XXIII**, 235–48

Walker, J 1991 *Secret Berwick: A photographer's impression*. Morpeth: Northumberland County Library

Walker, J 2006 *Berwick-upon-Tweed*. [Berwick-upon-Tweed]: Blackhall Press

Walker, J 2006 *By Net and Coble: Salmon fishing on the Tweed*. [Berwick-upon-Tweed]: Blackhall Press

William Whellan & Co 1855 *History, Topography and Directory of Northumberland*. London: Whittaker

White, W 1859 *Northumberland and the Border*, 2 edn. London: Chapman & Hall

Back cover
This strongly built door in the ramparts linked Dewar & Carmichael's granary with the quayside and was one of a series of public and private lanes and tunnels piercing the Quay Walls. Latterly goods passed through this doorway on a tramway.
[DP065153]

Other titles in the Informed Conservation series

Behind the Veneer: The South Shoreditch furniture trade and its buildings.
Joanna Smith and Ray Rogers, 2006. Product code 51204, ISBN 9781873592960

The Birmingham Jewellery Quarter: An introduction and guide.
John Cattell and Bob Hawkins, 2000. Product code 50205, ISBN 9781850747772

Bridport and West Bay: The buildings of the flax and hemp industry.
Mike Williams, 2006. Product code 51167, ISBN 9781873592861

Building a Better Society: Liverpool's historic institutional buildings.
Colum Giles, 2008. Product code 51332, ISBN 9781873592908

Built on Commerce: Liverpool's central business district.
Joseph Sharples and John Stonard, 2008. Product code 51331, ISBN 9781905624348

Built to Last? The buildings of the Northamptonshire boot and shoe industry.
Kathryn A Morrison with Ann Bond, 2004. Product code 50921, ISBN 9781873592793

Gateshead: Architecture in a changing English urban landscape.
Simon Taylor and David Lovie, 2004. Product code 52000, ISBN 9781873592762

Manchester's Northern Quarter.
Simon Taylor and Julian Holder, 2008. Product code 50946, ISBN 9781873592847

Manchester: The warehouse legacy – An introduction and guide.
Simon Taylor, Malcolm Cooper and P S Barnwell, 2002. Product code 50668, ISBN 9781873592670

Margate's Seaside Heritage.
Nigel Barker, Allan Brodie, Nick Dermott, Lucy Jessop and Gary Winter, 2007. Product code 51335, ISBN 9781905624669

Newcastle's Grainger Town: An urban renaissance.
Fiona Cullen and David Lovie, 2003. Product code 50811, ISBN 9781873592779

'One Great Workshop': The buildings of the Sheffield metal trades.
Nicola Wray, Bob Hawkins and Colum Giles, 2001. Product code 50214, ISBN 9781873592663

Ordinary Landscapes, Special Places: Anfield, Breckfield and the growth of Liverpool's suburbs.
Adam Menuge, 2008. Product code 51343, ISBN 9781873592892

Places of Health and Amusement: Liverpool's historic parks and gardens.
Katy Layton-Jones and Robert Lee, 2008. Product code 51333, ISBN 9781873592915

Religion and Place in Leeds.
John Minnis with Trevor Mitchell, 2007. Product code 51337, ISBN 9781905624485

Religion and Place: Liverpool's historic places of worship.
Sarah Brown and Peter de Figueiredo, 2008. Product code 51334, ISBN 9781873592885

Storehouses of Empire: Liverpool's historic warehouses.
Colum Giles and Bob Hawkins, 2004. Product code 50920, ISBN 9781873592809

Stourport-on-Severn: Pioneer town of the canal age.
Colum Giles, Keith Falconer, Barry Jones and Michael Taylor, 2007. Product code 51290, ISBN 9781905624362

Weymouth's Seaside Heritage.
Allan Brodie, Colin Ellis, David Stuart and Gary Winter, 2008. Product code 51429, ISBN 9781848020085

To order through EH Sales
Tel: 0845 458 9910
Fax: 0845 458 9912
Email: eh@centralbooks.com
Online bookshop: www.english-heritage.org.uk

Tweedmouth today

Selected buildings of interest

- ☐ Ecclesiastical
- ◐ Public
- ● Industrial
- ● Commercial

1. Meeting house (demolished)
2. Kingdom Hall, former Presbyterian Free Church
3. St Bartholomew's Church
4. Tweedmouth West First School
5. Tweed Flour Mill (Short's Mill)
6. Border Brewery
7. Tower Foundry (demolished)
8. Tweed Sawmills (Allan Bros)(demolished)
9. The Thatch PH
10. Tweedside Co-operative Society Ltd

Blackwell Road

Royal Tweed Bridge

Berwick Bridge

West End Road

West End

Union Park Road

Yard Heads

Ord Drive

Union Brae

Prince Edward Road

Yard Heads

Main Street

Tweed Dock

Osborne Road

Kiln Hill

Knowe Head

Church Road

River Tweed

Main Street

Tweed Dock Branch Railway

Mount Road

Goody Patchy

Carr Rock

North British Railway (Kelso & Tweedmouth Branch)

Shielfield Park

Etal Road

Former stn

Dock Road

Howick Tce

Falloden Tce

Billendean Road

Northumberland Road

Crescent

Askew

Billendean Road

0   100   300 m
0 100   900 ft